# Bullying

# Other Books in the Social Issues Firsthand Series:

SOCIAL ISSUES
FIRSTHAND

# Bullying

*Norah Piehl, Book Editor*

**GREENHAVEN PRESS**
*A part of Gale, Cengage Learning*

GALE
CENGAGE Learning™

Detroit • New York • San Francisco • New Haven, Conn • Waterville, Maine • London

GALE
CENGAGE Learning™

Christine Nasso, *Publisher*
Elizabeth Des Chenes, *Managing Editor*

© 2009 Greenhaven Press, a part of Gale, Cengage Learning.

Gale and Greenhaven Press are registered trademarks used herein under license.

*For more information, contact:*
Greenhaven Press
27500 Drake Rd.
Farmington Hills, MI 48331-3535
Or you can visit our Internet site at gale.cengage.com

For product information and technology assistance, contact us at

Gale Customer Support, 1-800-877-4253
For permission to use material from this text or product, submit all requests online at www.cengage.com/permissions

Further permissions questions can be emailed to permissionrequest@cengage.com

Articles in Greenhaven Press anthologies are often edited for length to meet page requirements. In addition, original titles of these works are changed to clearly present the main thesis and to explicitly indicate the author's opinion. Every effort is made to ensure that Greenhaven Press accurately reflects the original intent of the authors. Every effort has been made to trace the owners of copyrighted material.

Cover photograph reproduced by © Pixland/Corbis.

**LIBRARY OF CONGRESS CATALOGING-IN-PUBLICATION DATA**

Bullying / Norah Piehl, book editor.
      p. cm. -- (Social issues firsthand)
      Includes bibliographical references and index.
      ISBN 978-0-7377-3833-9 (hardcover)
      1. Bullying. I. Piehl, Norah.
      BF637.B85B843 2009
      302.3--dc22

                                                  2008049413

Printed in the United States of America
1 2 3 4 5 6 7 13 12 11 10 09

# Contents

## Chapter 1: Voices of Victims and Perpetrators

# Chapter 3: Overcoming the Effects of Bullying

# Foreword

Social issues are often viewed in abstract terms. Pressing challenges such as poverty, homelessness, and addiction are viewed as problems to be defined and solved. Politicians, social scientists, and other experts engage in debates about the extent of the problems, their causes, and how best to remedy them. Often overlooked in these discussions is the human dimension of the issue. Behind every policy debate over poverty, homelessness, and substance abuse, for example, are real people struggling to make ends meet, to survive life on the streets, and to overcome addiction to drugs and alcohol. Their stories are ubiquitous and compelling. They are the stories of everyday people—perhaps your own family members or friends—and yet they rarely influence the debates taking place in state capitols, the national Congress, or the courts.

The disparity between the public debate and private experience of social issues is well illustrated by looking at the topic of poverty. Each year the U.S. Census Bureau establishes a poverty threshold. A household with an income below the threshold is defined as poor, while a household with an income above the threshold is considered able to live on a basic subsistence level. For example, in 2003 a family of two was considered poor if its income was less than $12,015; a family of four was defined as poor if its income was less than $18,810. Based on this system, the bureau estimates that 35.9 million Americans (12.5 percent of the population) lived below the poverty line in 2003, including 12.9 million children below the age of eighteen.

Commentators disagree about what these statistics mean. Social activists insist that the huge number of officially poor Americans translates into human suffering. Even many families that have incomes above the threshold, they maintain, are likely to be struggling to get by. Other commentators insist that the statistics exaggerate the problem of poverty in the United States. Compared to people in developing countries, they point out, most so-called poor families have a high quality of life. As stated by journalist Fidelis Iyebote, "Cars are owned by 70 percent of 'poor' households. . . . Color televisions belong to 97 percent of the 'poor' [and] videocassette recorders belong to nearly 75 percent. . . . Sixty-four percent have microwave ovens, half own a stereo system, and over a quarter possess an automatic dishwasher."

However, this debate over the poverty threshold and what it means is likely irrelevant to a person living in poverty. Simply put, poor people do not need the government to tell them whether they are poor. They can see it in the stack of bills they cannot pay. They are aware of it when they are forced to choose between paying rent or buying food for their children. They become painfully conscious of it when they lose their homes and are forced to live in their cars or on the streets. Indeed, the written stories of poor people define the meaning of poverty more vividly than a government bureaucracy could ever hope to. Narratives composed by the poor describe losing jobs due to injury or mental illness, depict horrific tales of childhood abuse and spousal violence, recount the loss of friends and family members. They evoke the slipping away of social supports and government assistance, the descent into substance abuse and addiction, the harsh realities of life on the streets. These are the perspectives on poverty that are too often omitted from discussions over the extent of the problem and how to solve it.

Greenhaven Press's *Social Issues Firsthand* series provides a forum for the often-overlooked human perspectives on society's most divisive topics of debate. Each volume focuses on one social issue and presents a collection of ten to sixteen narratives by those who have had personal involvement with the topic. Extra care has been taken to include a diverse range of perspectives. For example, in the volume on adoption, readers will find the stories of birth parents who have made an adoption plan, adoptive parents, and adoptees themselves. After exposure to these varied points of view, the reader will have a clearer understanding that adoption is an intense, emotional experience full of joyous highs and painful lows for all concerned.

The debate surrounding embryonic stem cell research illustrates the moral and ethical pressure that the public brings to bear on the scientific community. However, while nonexperts often criticize scientists for not considering the potential negative impact of their work, ironically the public's reaction against such discoveries can produce harmful results as well. For example, although the outcry against embryonic stem cell research in the United States has resulted in fewer embryos being destroyed, those with Parkinson's, such as actor Michael J. Fox, have argued that prohibiting the development of new stem cell lines ultimately will prevent a timely cure for the disease that is killing Fox and thousands of others.

Each book in the series contains several features that enhance its usefulness, including an in-depth introduction, an annotated table of contents, bibliographies for further research, a list of organizations to contact, and a thorough index. These elements—combined with the poignant voices of people touched by tragedy and triumph—make the Social Issues Firsthand series a valuable resource for research on today's topics of political discussion.

# Introduction

As a preteen, Gabrielle (Gabe) Ford was a gifted ballet dancer, on her way to a promising career in dance. Then, at the age of twelve, Gabe was struck with Friedreich's ataxia, a neuromuscular disease similar to muscular dystrophy. The disease affected her balance, coordination, and speech, putting an end to her dreams of becoming a dancer. That disappointment, however, was only the beginning—when Gabe moved to a new school shortly after developing the disease, she was relentlessly teased, mocked, and harassed by other students for her awkward speech and uncoordinated movements. As a result, this bright young woman, who had previously loved the spotlight, spent most of her high school years hiding at home, desperate to avoid the bullies who targeted her at school.

Unfortunately, Gabe's story is an all-too-common one. Anecdotes similar to Gabe's abound in online discussion forums, support groups, and blogs, but researchers are just beginning to understand the many links between school bullying and physical and mental disabilities. Surprisingly, this recent research shows that the relationship is significantly more complicated than the stereotypical image of a big, tough bully preying on a defenseless, physically weak victim.

## Easy Targets

Research on bullying has been on the rise in recent years, ever since a wave of school shootings in the late 1990s (the Columbine, Colorado, case being the most notorious) shed new light on the seriousness of bullying and redefined the problem as a potential public health and safety issue. According to a 2003 study by the National Center for Education Statistics, 25 percent of elementary and high school students and 40 percent of middle school students in the general population report being bullied at least once per week.

Rates of bullying among the disabled population are, according to numerous studies, significantly higher. Physical disabilities—including deafness, cerebral palsy, muscular dystrophy, scoliosis, obesity, and partial paralysis—result in high rates of both physical and emotional bullying. Children with speech disabilities, particularly stuttering, are especially at risk; a 1999 study found that 83 percent of adults who had stammered as children reported being victims of regular bullying. Students with mental retardation are prime targets for bullying, according to a 2004 article in the *Journal of Instructional Psychology*, partly because they "lack the awareness to realize that potentially dangerous situations are developing."

## A More Complicated Picture

These statistics about the victimization of those with physical disabilities and mental retardation probably do not come as much of a surprise. The picture grows fuzzier, though, when researchers look at issues surrounding those with learning disabilities and emotional disorders. Sometimes, as with autism spectrum disorders, the characteristics of these disabilities match up with the typical profile of a bullying victim—passivity, lack of humor, social isolation—and result in higher rates of bullying victimization. In the case of attention-deficit/hyperactivity disorder (ADHD) and learning disabilities, however, the affected child might demonstrate a variety of behaviors. According to the *Journal of Instructional Psychology*, some children with learning disabilities have poor social skills and are "ostracized by their peers," resulting in higher rates of bullying victimization. Other students with learning disabilities, however, act out their frustrations with aggressive, antisocial behavior—and are actually more likely to become bullies themselves. Similarly, a 2003 report showed that students with ADHD are more likely to be bullied *and* more likely to become bullies themselves, as their unhappiness and anxieties often manifest themselves in aggression toward other students.

## Finding Solutions

Virtually all students, teachers, administrators, and parents agree that a culture of bullying and victimization should not be tolerated in the school setting. The reviews of school-sponsored antibullying initiatives and interventions, however, are mixed at best, particularly when the complicated issues of disability awareness and sensitivity are added to the mix. Several studies agree that including students with disabilities in the general curriculum, rather than segregating them in special education programs, is one factor in reducing a culture of labeling and separation that often results in increased social stratification, cliques, and bullying.

An inclusive environment, however, is not the only solution. Because students take so many behavioral cues from authority figures, "the quality of youth peer cultures is largely determined by adults," according to a 2001 article in the journal *Reclaiming Children and Youth*. Adults in the academic environment must be positive and emotionally involved as well as authoritative, setting boundaries and imposing consistent consequences for inappropriate behavior.

According to recommendations from the U.S. Department of Education, disability awareness and sensitivity training—for both adults and students—should also be part of any school-wide antibullying initiative, and schools should develop disability harassment policies in addition to bullying prevention policies. On a more personal level, parents and other adults who work with children with disabilities should counsel students on an individual level, helping children identify and label bullying and reassuring children that bullying is not their fault. Often, according to education specialist Jocelyn Taylor, students with autism spectrum disorders can benefit from social skills training that can help minimize a child's victim-like behaviors and characteristics. Similarly, children with ADHD and learning disabilities—whether acting as bullies or victims—can profit from individual counseling and training that helps students redirect self-defeating or aggressive impulses.

## Drastic Measures

But what happens if these interventions and initiatives do not solve the problem? For disabled students who are consistently victimized, there can be legal recourse. Bullying of the disabled may cross the line into "disability harassment," which is illegal under the 1973 Rehabilitation Act and the 1990 Americans with Disabilities Act. Disabled students, including Taya Haugstad, who suffers from cerebral palsy, and Billy Wolfe, who has learning disabilities, have successfully sued their bullies and their school districts in federal court for harassment and negligence. Disabled students may be at greater risk of getting bullied—but fortunately they also are provided with protections not necessarily available to the general public.

## A Happy Ending

As for Gabe Ford, her story proves that often, disabled students are able to find sources of comfort and strength even without taking perpetrators to court. Gabe, who was lonely and anxious following her retreat from high school social life, asked for a dog to keep her company. Not long afterward, Gabe's coonhound, Izzy, was coincidentally diagnosed with a serious muscular ailment similar to Gabe's own. As Gabe accompanied Izzy to her veterinarian visits, she gradually grew braver and more confident about her own abilities. After the duo was profiled on TV's Animal Planet network in 2001, the pair's newfound fame translated into a series of antibullying, motivational speaking engagements and even a forthcoming book. Now Gabe, whose dreams of stardom were derailed by disability and whose fears of bullying drove her to silence, has found her way back to the spotlight—and to self-confidence.

# CHAPTER 1

# Voices of Victims
# and Perpetrators

# Teasing and Bullying Start Early

*Jane Katch*

*Many people tend to associate bullying with the late elementary and middle school years. However, as preschool teacher Jane Katch notes in her essay, often the groundwork for bullying is laid many years earlier. In her story, Katch describes a confrontation that happened in her preschool classroom as a result of one younger boy failing to follow the "rules" of play set by his slightly older classmates.*

*As the children relate the events that led one boy to tell another, "We don't like you," Katch reflects on her own childhood and young adulthood, when she often had trouble fitting in. Her own background—as well as her belief in fostering an inclusive classroom—makes her inclined to step in when she witnesses early examples of bullying and exclusion. On the other hand, this dedicated preschool teacher knows that she needs to let each student find his or her own place in the community of the classroom. As she points out, even at this early stage, bullying and its remedies are complicated.*

*Jane Katch is a veteran early childhood educator and the author of two books:* Under Deadman's Skin: Discovering the Meaning of Children's Violent Play *and* They Don't Like Me: Lessons on Bullying and Teasing from a Preschool Classroom.

"We don't like you."

Hearing those harsh words, I look up quickly from the art table, where I am mixing the morning's paints. It is only the first week of school but I know they come from five-year-old Toby, already the vortex of conflict in my class.

From other children I may hear, "I won't invite you to my birthday party," or "You're not my friend," pronouncements intended to persuade another child to play a game or give up a toy. But Toby's statement has a more deadly message: *you have already been rejected by the group of important people in this classroom.*

In my first years of teaching, I ignored such statements, fearing that if I paid attention to them I would make the ostracized child even more uncomfortable. In the next years, I lectured the children about the importance of kindness and inclusion. But now I feel a need to understand: why does a young child, just becoming aware of the existence of the group, feel such a strong need to keep another child out?

## Rejection

"Let's go smash his guy," Toby tells Sean and Russell, who are sitting near him at the table, as Toby hits four-year-old Noah's small plastic truck driver with his own.

Noah slowly stands up and walks silently to the block area, his shoulders slumped and his face impassive. Rejection by his favorite group of older boys can drive him away, even from the red, blue, and yellow blocks with wheels that attach with a black screwdriver.

"What's wrong?" I ask the three boys who are sitting around the sides of the table. They avoid my eyes and my question. I look at the empty chair and then at Noah.

"They don't like me," he whispers.

"Toby's being mean to him," Sean says at last, chewing on the cuff of his red long-sleeved T-shirt.

"Why did you say, 'We don't like you'?" I ask Toby, who pushes the wisps of dark hair away from his face. Toby has a big boy's haircut, professionally trimmed along the sides and back. Noah, in contrast, still has the unruly, honey-brown curls of a younger boy. They stare at me blankly.

"Share the toys," Timmy, the youngest child in my class, suggests, remembering that adults usually approve of this solution to conflict.

## Role Playing

"Come back here a moment, Noah," I say. He returns slowly, not knowing what I might have in mind. I hand each boy one of the plastic truck drivers. "Show me what happened in your game," I tell them. "Pretend you're playing it again."

After a pause, Toby begins. "I want to get some more power," he says, speaking for his girl truck driver.

Toby always wants more. He wants the tallest block house for his stuffed animals, the steepest incline for his car track, and the longest tail on his dragon painting. Often he's so preoccupied with getting the most, he doesn't get around to playing before it's time to clean up and have a snack.

"She's the boss bad guy," he explains now, handing her to Russell, who is sitting across the table. Russell has gel keeping the front of his red hair in a flip, just like his older brother, who walked him into the room this morning. Russell accepts the figure and puts her in a small plastic box that once held the treasure for a toy pirate set. "This is taking all of her power!" he says excitedly, as he takes the girl out of the box. Taking power from the boss bad girl seems to please all four boys and is clearly not the source of the conflict.

"What happened next?" I ask.

Noah puts his truck driver in front of him on the table. "I just put this down for a minute," he says softly.

Toby picks it up quickly, puts it in the treasure box, and closes the lid. "I took up your energy," Toby tells the figure when he opens the box. "Now you can't move."

"You can't! You can't!" Noah protests quietly, his large dark eyes looking worried.

"That sucks up power!" Toby explains to him. "This is a *real* game," he says, adding legitimacy to his argument. I am not sure where the original real game ends and the reenactment begins, but I think that if I am patient we may soon find out what led to Toby's rejection of Noah.

## Changing the Rules

"You can't suck up my power!" Noah tells him earnestly. "Because this is an ice thing." He puts one finger on a small red block. "When I push this switch, there it goes! I turned into ice *before* you sucked up my energy."

I am impressed with Noah's new invention, designed on the spot to block Toby's power. But Toby is not pleased.

"No! You don't have ice power now!" Toby argues. He is in the game, forgetting this is a reenactment.

"Yeah!" Russell agrees.

Toby stops abruptly and looks at me.

"That's when he said we don't like him," Sean explains, examining the dark, wet spot he's been chewing at the end of his sleeve.

## Bringing Back Memories

These four words threaten to suck my power, too, bringing back a string of memories beginning in kindergarten. I was the youngest in my class when the teacher said, "Put your chair in a circle." I took the command literally, searching all over the floor for a circle in which to place my chair, puzzled that all the other children seemed to know where to go. In fourth grade, the girls in the popular group all held hands in a line at recess while I wondered how they came to be the chosen ones. By sixth grade, I knew enough to pretend to have a crush on one of the boys, just to sound like the other girls, who already had the beginnings of breasts and changing hormones. I still dream that I am at a cocktail party, finally looking great in a slinky black dress, only to look down and realize I am wearing the red tie shoes of my childhood, caught again in the act of pretending to belong.

I want my classroom to be a respite, a place of safety. But more than that, I want each child to have the opportunity to belong, to learn to be a valued member of the group.

## Finding a Place

I would like to help Noah find the place he wants among these older boys. But I also know I must not alienate them during these important first weeks of school. My fours seem so innocent; they just want a good toy, preferably one with wheels, and plenty of time to explore with it. These fives, who have already told us they are six, are involved in a separate drama of power and status. They have older brothers and sisters, and they know how real big kids talk.

Noah is the bridge between these two groups. Unlike Timmy, he is no longer satisfied with just his favorite toy. Having become aware that there is a social group, he wants, more than anything, to be accepted by it. He is willing to argue the relative merits of ice power and energy-sucking machines, but Toby's words, "We don't like you," rejection in the name of the group, make him give up and walk away.

"This is complicated," I say, "and I want to understand it. Toby, are you angry because you took the energy from Noah's guy first, before he tried to stop you with his ice power?"

"That's when we said, 'We don't like you.'" Toby agrees. "He wasn't playing by the rules."

"Compel-cated, compel-cated," Russell sings softly in the background, enjoying the sound of my long word.

Now that I understand the annoyance of the older boys toward the younger child who was not following the conventions of their game, I feel more sympathetic to them. But how was it decided that Noah's figure was the one to lose power? And must he agree or leave?

## Learning New Language

"When someone plays in a way that you think is unfair, what can you do?" I ask.

Brooke and Gwynn have been listening from the art table nearby.

"Don't say, 'I don't like you,'" Brooke tells them. "That's not a nice word to say because it hurts their feelings."

"Did that hurt your feelings?" I ask Noah. He nods, his eyes large and solemn.

"You can't say, 'You can't play,'" Brooke reminds Toby. This is a rule in our school, which we adopted after the teachers read Vivian Paley's book by that name. We agreed with Paley that we wanted our young children to learn social skills by being included in the group. When a young child is rejected year after year, he or she does not have the opportunity to develop and practice the ability to become a constructive group member, an important foundation of learning at our school. I introduce the rule the first week of September and we discuss the ramifications all year.

"You can say, 'That's not fair,'" Brooke prompts Noah.

"Or, 'That's not fun,'" Gwynn adds.

"Or, 'That's not good.'"

"Or, 'That's not nice.'" The children like the rhythm of Brooke's words.

"Then you'd be bossy," Toby objects.

"If you say, 'please,' that wouldn't be bossy," Gwynn tells him.

"Let's notice when telling someone how you feel seems bossy and when it helps the problem," I say. "We'll talk about this again."

"Compel-cated, compel-cated," Russell whispers in the background.

# Confessions of a Boy Dancer

*Rhee Gold*

*Bullies frequently target those who do not fit established norms of behavior. As Rhee Gold notes in his essay, male dancers, despite being involved in an activity that's just as athletically demanding as football or basketball, are often the brunt of teasing and confrontation based on stereotyped perceptions of their masculinity and sexuality.*

*Gold, an adult dancer who shares his own horror stories of growing up being bullied for being different, advises parents and dance teachers to be aware of the embarrassing taunts and torments their male students may be secretly undergoing, and to recognize this added stress on male dancers as they attempt to excel at their chosen pursuit.*

*Rhee Gold also advises talented male students to stick with their dreams and reminds them that things will get better as they get older. Gold himself survived bullying to become a leader in the dance industry, publishing a magazine for dance studio owners and writing a definitive book on teaching dance. In addition, Gold serves as a motivational speaker through Project Motivate, a program that encourages dance teachers to serve as mentors, resources, and inspirations for their students.*

Earlier this year, I was helping a dance-teacher friend prepare a few of her dancers for a title competition. The dancers were to be scored on a talent presentation as well as a judge's interview. My job was to prepare each of the kids for the dreaded interview. This was not the first time I had done this: I have been part of more than a dozen mock interviews over the past couple of years.

The first couple of dancers—girls—went through the process smoothly. The third one was a 15-year-old boy who had trained with this particular teacher since the age of 3. I had seen him perform many times and I knew he was excellent. He's the kind of kid who always stands out, not only because he is a strong technician but because he gives the audience that "I love what I do" feeling whenever he hits the stage.

He did very well with the first few questions, as I expected from such a personable kid. Then I said, "Tell me what your male friends think about your dancing." All of a sudden there was silence. His confidence level went from one hundred to one. At first he started to ramble without really answering the question, so I asked it again. Within seconds, he was crying.

He started telling me that he didn't want to go to school anymore because he was constantly being harassed and he was actually beaten up several times—all because he danced. He said his classmates—boys and girls alike—were always calling him a fag. He was dealing with this day in and day out, and it had obviously had a major emotional effect on him.

Instead of continuing with the interview, I gave him a pep talk and tried to explain that the kids who were making fun of him could be jealous, or didn't comprehend how athletic dance really was. I encouraged him to keep dancing because I thought he had what it took to make it. We ended our time together with a laugh or two, but I could tell he was extremely troubled.

As I was driving home, I couldn't get this kid out of my mind. I, too, had danced from age 3 on. I had no choice: My mother was my dance teacher and my father was in show business. And I had been through the same torment this kid was enduring. I can remember sneaking out the back door of my junior high school to avoid the bullies who would think nothing of giving me a punch or two and call me a fag every time they had the opportunity.

## Living in Fear

I remember one morning when I was walking to school: I arrived at the front door wearing a winter coat with a hood. One of the kids, who I knew was trouble, walked up to me and pulled my hood off my head to spit in my face as he called me a fag. Another time, I was walking home from school and the same kid picked up a huge two-by-four and whacked me in the stomach several times as he called me unprintable names.

When I got to high school the situation was worse; like the boy in the interview, I didn't want to go to school either. But, through it all, there was never a question of whether I would continue dancing, because it was in my blood and I loved it. My issue was how I was going to keep myself from getting beaten up or from being brought down by the name-calling. Somehow, I managed.

When I was about 16, our family did an interview with the local newspaper. It was a story about the Gold family and how we all were into show business. Instead of being excited about my picture being in the paper. I was in fear that this article would be another opportunity to remind all the bullies that I danced. And it did. The article appeared, and so did an entirely new round of harassment.

I never talked to my parents about the situation: actually, I never discussed it with anyone for more than twenty years. I think I was embarrassed, and I didn't want anyone to know about it. Why I was embarrassed I don't know; it was just one of those things you push to the back of your mind. It was the interview with this boy that brought it all back to me—not just the memories, but the feelings as well.

## Established Stereotypes

You would think that the twenty-first century would bring a new perception of male dancers. They are everywhere, from Gap commercials to MTV, and they are portrayed in a very masculine way. So why are boys who dance still going through the persecution? I believe it's the adults in the kid's life who influence this kind of behavior or thinking. They are the ones I went to school with, and they still think that dancing is a "sissy" thing for guys to do. They pass their prejudices on to their children, creating an entirely new generation of kids who make fun of boys who dance.

Dance teachers and parents need to realize that their male dancers may be suffering through this torment: the kids may not bring it up because they are embarassed, as I was. It might be a good thing to discuss at the studio or at home. It could be through rap sessions with all the dancers or one-on-one conversations with the boys. They need to know that they are not alone, that there are others who deal with the same issue. Just talking about it could make a world of difference. Another option might be for the parent and child to approach his teachers or school principal about the problem. In certain situations, counseling may be appropriate.

Often, dance teachers see young male dancers who show enormous potential and love dancing but who quit at the age of 12 or 13. My guess is that it's because they cannot take the abuse. I wonder—how many great dancers have we lost in this way?

Hard as it may be, I encourage young male dancers to stick it out. I have no regrets; I think it was the harassment that motivated me to become what I am today. Now I realize it was a unique motivation for me. I went on to perform all over the country and even became Mr. Dance of America in 1982. Today I direct one of the largest dance production companies in the world; I am a past president of Dance Masters of America; I serve as a motivational speaker for dance educators; and I write for *Dance Magazine*. Not bad for a kid who could have given it all up just to stop the torment.

By the way, the last time I saw the kid who spit in my face and hit me with the two-by-four, he was working at the local gas station.

# The Cold Shoulder

*Carolyn Magner*

*Carolyn Magner's daughter was bright, athletic, friendly, and popular—at least until midway through seventh grade, when girls at her new private school suddenly, and cruelly, turned from friends to foes. From online smear campaigns to brutal exclusion, her daughter's classmates staged a surprisingly well-orchestrated and damaging effort to belittle and torment their former friend.*

*As a mother, Magner was in a difficult position. Never one to micromanage her daughter's academic or social life, she was reluctant to swoop in and try to impose changes, especially when doing so might actually make the situation worse. What's more, in those feelings of helplessness and hopelessness, Magner began to question her own parenting abilities and approaches, wondering whether she could have made different choices that would have resulted in better outcomes for her hurting daughter. Ultimately, Magner and her husband decided that the best approach was simply to support their daughter, watching for signs of depression and despair and offering reassurance that things could get better.*

*Carolyn Magner is an author of books for children, an advice columnist, and a writer whose articles and personal essays have appeared frequently in Salon.com,* The Christian Science Monitor, *and* Family Circle, *among other publications.*

This time last year, my happy, friendly seventh-grade daughter was voted off the island. The stars aligned, the dice rolled, the ballots were cast and she was "it." She went from being a member of the "in crowd" to becoming its designated exile. She was talked about, hated, despised, not invited, ridiculed, but mostly, most cruelly, ignored.

Carolyn Magner, "When They Were Bad," Salon.com, October 9, 2000. This article first appeared in Salon.com at http://www.salon.com. An online version remains in the Salon archives. Reprinted with permission.

"I don't exist," she explained to me softly.

"Why?" I yelled to the heavens. "Why you? Why me, the mother of you? What have we done?"

I found out about the smear campaign when I read a batch of saved e-mails my daughter left open on the family computer. She'd never done that before, so I figured she wanted me to read them. She did and I did and it hurt. The electronic missives went beyond mean to breathtakingly evil and they were attached to extensive buddy lists. It seemed that everyone knew about this except me.

## Feeling Hopeless

I should have known. The phone never rang anymore, my daughter's grades were dropping and she had a hard time getting up in the morning. I constantly asked what was up. Finally, e-mails in hand, I asked again, "Are the girls mad at you?" She stared at me with old, sad eyes and said, "Yes."

What to do? Press for information? Sympathize? Call the mothers? Or do I do what I want to do and murder a bunch of girls for being spiteful adolescents?

Sound bitter? Well, I was a girl once. I survived—just barely—being left out of a chick clique. I know that sisterhood can suck. Plus, I've read Margaret Atwood's *Cat's Eye* and Mary Pipher's *Reviving Ophelia*, and I know that raising girls is not for the fainthearted. But even an educated veteran of girlie bullying doesn't think it's going to happen to her daughter. And when it does, she realizes that the only thing to do is hope, pray and stick pins in dolls—whatever gets you through.

I sought counsel from a wise and crusty high school teacher who advised that I stay out of it, adding, "What doesn't kill her, makes her stronger." OK, but what if it did kill her? It crossed my mind more than once when I couldn't wake my daughter in the morning. My heart racing, I would bend over to feel her morning breath on my cheek until finally her eyes would open and she'd begin telling me all the reasons she couldn't go to school.

The car pool line was the worst part of the day. I would pull up to see my daughter standing alone on the curb, scanning cars with wounded eyes. The rest of the girls huddled a regulation 10 feet behind her. Every time one of them climbed into a car, the rest would wave goodbye, making phone call hand signals and typing motions signifying, "Call me, e-mail me, we'll get right back on it as soon as we get home."

My daughter would walk slowly to our car, a tight smile glued on her face. She'd get in, lock the doors and turn her body toward the window. Then she would cry great gulping sobs of despair and misery and hopelessness. Sometimes, I'd want to laugh, sputtering something like, "Oh baby, if you think this is bad. . . ." Mostly I'd grip the steering wheel in cold, white rage.

## One Month Later

I gave it a month. I promised my daughter that the clique would wear itself out by Thanksgiving. I was wrong. Fueled by e-mail and instant messages, the campaign intensified and the fall semester crept by in excrutiating real time. My daughter's transgressions were never completely defined. She'd beg for explanations: "Am I mean? Am I ugly? Did I say or do something wrong?" But there was never an answer. Her tormentors would roll their eyes and sigh as if to say: "If you don't know, then you are more dense than we thought."

Even the fringe girls, those not quite in the clique, started avoiding my daughter. Under strict orders from the reigning queens to not speak to, look at or, God help you, sit near the victim, they complied until finally, the cheese stood alone.

I find myself in a group of can-do moms, who tend to make things happen—and stop happening. I've watched them storm into the principal's office demanding different teachers and disputing grades. I've had mothers try to enlist me in various fix-it campaigns, from banning science projects to changing reading programs. I have declined to participate, mostly because I've always been afraid to tempt the fates. So I don't interfere. I never call other mothers or make appointments with principals. I try to stay out of my children's quarrels and petty grievances. I don't believe in fixing science projects any more than I believe in fixing problems. And, while I would have tried anything during this debacle, I didn't want to make things worse.

My husband, meanwhile, couldn't get over it: "Why do they do this?" he demanded again and again. "Because it gives them power, sickening, glorious, intoxicating power over another human being," I would say. "They don't think she's really suffering. They don't imagine her pain. They are just damn glad it's not them and so they participate. They instigate. They fuel the fire, fan the flames and all of it bonds them closer. Sometimes they are sickened by it, their conscience aches and they put themselves in the victim's Nikes. Eventually, they convince themselves she deserves it. And ultimately, they are terrified of becoming the next victim. So, they do what they have to."

## Seeking Answers

I couldn't determine who was the queen. I'd pick one and then it would be another one who was uncommonly cruel that day. I kept thinking it would end. It didn't. I lectured constantly: "When you come out of this, you won't be the same. You will never participate in this kind of thing. You will be stronger, you will be tougher, you will be nicer to those less smart, pretty and talented than you." She'd nod but I know she didn't believe me. Heck, I didn't believe me.

I read up on warning signals of teenage depression. I went into chat rooms where teens poured out their angst and suggested ways to kill themselves. I locked up the booze, threw out prescription medications, made sure she ate, watched to see if she swallowed, followed her to the bathroom. I slowly lost myself. I avoided friends, didn't go to parties and suffered along with her. How long could it last? How long could *we* last?

I bargained with God. I told him I'd go to church more, pray harder and keep more commandments if he'd take this from her. I blamed myself. I hadn't hosted enough sleepovers. I didn't play tennis with the other mothers. I didn't go out to lunch with the ladies. I worked too much. I wasn't a popular mother.

## Small Kindnesses

There were kindnesses along the way. Random phone calls from other mothers. One friend sent a plant with a note saying, "By the time this blooms, it will be over." Childhood friends from the other school in town started dropping by, calling. A track coach asked her to run for the team. A school guidance counselor asked her to volunteer at a crisis center, filing papers and making coffee. I was pitifully grateful for each of them. A truism struck home with staggering force: "You find out who your friends are."

These gestures provided the first rays of light in a long, dark stretch. Volunteer work gave my daughter something to focus on other than her own misery; track made her part of a team. Old friends provided evidence that she was not unlovable.

The holidays arrived and things were less than merry. My daughter didn't get invited to Christmas parties; her name wasn't on any gift swap lists. She stayed close to my side, rarely venturing out. We both thought the spring semester would be better; but just in case, we started talking about switching schools, even though she'd been at this one for less than nine months.

## A Good Decision Turned Bad

We had made the decision to try private school after sixth grade, mostly because the public middle school was plagued with problems related to overcrowding and discipline. My daughter had lots of friends at the private school; they were in dance together and played softball in the same league. The plan was to enjoy these friendships at school, along with small classes and more athletic opportunities.

And the transfer worked like a charm. My daughter had a tight group of friends upon arrival at the private school—they picked up where they left off during the summer. But when she was arbitrarily exiled a couple of months into the school year, it occured to me, as I wrote the spring tuition check, that I was paying big bucks for this horror show.

My daughter started spending time with girls from the other school. I started to go out some, see old friends, have dates with my husband. Life started to feel a little more normal, less of an ordeal. My daughter started to lose her black circles and haunted look. I stopped waking in the night. The season of hell began to run its course, like a bad case of the flu. But none of us were unscathed. Not my daughter, not me and not the perps.

Finally, despite the signs of détente, my daughter decided to quit the private school and go to the public school. The decision gave her something to hold on to, something to negate the feelings of hopelessness. An end was in sight. All of the messy social and economic issues dogging the public schools seemed puny compared to the ugly motives behind the private school freeze-out. I worried briefly that changing schools was a cowardly quick fix, but the decision felt right as soon as we made it.

## Valuable Lessons

Strangely, the girls were shocked by my daughter's decision to flee. Prompted by teachers and parents, they tentatively asked her why she was leaving. Nobody thought it had gone as far as it had. My daughter had done the stoic thing—held her head high and kept her tears in check. Her response to their bizarre expressions of concern was equally calm: "I'm outta here," she said. "I'm leaving you to torture each other."

A year later, my daughter's life is entirely different. She is happy and busy with friends, school work and activities. One of the former torturers is now being tortured. She calls my daughter and cries mournfully. I watch, fascinated, as my daughter murmurs sympathy, invites this onetime foe to spend the night, offers her a shoulder to cry on. How can she forgive so easily? Or was forgiveness the most valuable lesson? Perhaps, like the teacher so strangely predicted, it ends up being a good thing, something that makes her tougher, better, stronger in the long run.

I know I'm different. Not tougher, not stronger but changed somehow. It has finally sunk in. There is no immunization against hurt. There is no protection against cruelty. For all the things I can do for her, saving my daughter from life's hard twists is not one of them. Tough lesson all the way around.

Furthermore, if it's really the worst thing that ever happens to her, she'll indeed be lucky.

# Bullied to Death

*Rochelle Sides*

*Sometimes victims of incessant bullying grow so desperate that they feel they have lost all hope. Suicide among bullying victims is such a staggeringly common phenomenon that it has even coined a new term: "bullycide." According to some statistics, one child or teen attempts suicide every thirty minutes as a direct result of chronic bullying.*

*Corinne Wilson was one of those teenagers. She took her own life in 2004 at the age of thirteen. According to this essay written by her mother, Corinne had endured exclusion, taunts, and verbal abuse from other girls for several years before committing suicide. As in many other stories of female bullying, Corinne's primary attackers were also her best friends, at the center of her social life. When these so-called friends finally turned on her in one particularly cruel campaign, Corinne made a desperate—and tragic—call for help.*

*After Corinne's suicide, her mother, Rochelle Sides, became an antibullying activist. Sides used Corinne's experience to help pass the first antibullying law in Texas and now, as the codirector of Bully Police USA, she works to pass similar laws in all other states. Sides also speaks about her experience and Corinne's tragedy to school groups, community forums, and the media. Corinne's story is collected with those of other teens who took their own lives in response to bullying in a book,* Bullycide in America.

Corinne Celice Wilson was born on Monday, September 30, 1991, at 2:06 P.M. She is the youngest of four children and the only girl. She was the most beautiful baby with big blue eyes and blonde curly hair. From the day she was born she was an amazing child. I know that every mother says that,

Rochelle Sides, "Corinne's Story," JaredStory.com, Reproduced by permission.

but she was so bright and full of personality. She did everything early, said her first word at 8 months, walked by 11 months. I should have known then what was in store for me, but as a young mother of four I just thought it was because she was trying to keep up with her older brothers.

A few months before Corinne was 2 her biological father and I separated and later divorced. I met the man Corinne knew as her daddy when she was barely 3. We all moved to Texas in 1995. Corinne seemed to blossom under all of the love that my husband's family gave her, especially her Grandma Jewel, who fell madly in love with Corinne from the first day, as most people did that met her. That all changed when we moved to Rockdale, Texas in 2000. She had trouble from the first day; she missed her old school and friends and didn't feel as if she fit in here.

## Not Part of the Team

I thought that if she played a sport, that would help her to meet people. Unfortunately, it made it worse. It was Corinne's first year playing softball, and she was placed on a team of girls that had played for a considerable amount of time. They teased her relentlessly about her inability to play. She would cry after every practice.

I spoke to the coach about it and it seemed to let up, but they continued to exclude her at practice, which followed through to school. Corinne would periodically come home from school crying, saying, "No one likes me, I hate it here." I would tell her to try to be nice to one person every day and soon she would have a friend. It seemed to work; she made a friend and they seemed inseparable. However, that is when the trouble started for us, as Corinne started changing her personality to match her new friend's. My husband and I thought it was a phase. It came to a head when Corinne and this girl got into trouble when they were at the girl's house. Her father and I ended the relationship, so we thought.

## A New Kind of Pain

For some reason this girl had a hold on Corinne that we could not break. Corinne did make other friends, but they all included this girl. This continued with not much problem for the next year and half. Corinne was now in the 6th grade and really starting to become a beautiful young girl. Boys were interested in her and vice versa. I think that is where the bullying began; these girls were not nearly as pretty as Corinne and became jealous. Corinne was also excelling in academics as well. At first they would exclude her, make her cry, then make up. Then they started to tell Corinne she was fat and her hair was frizzy and make fun of her one day, then befriend her the next. Corinne was so confused. Over the summer of her 6th grade going into 7th grade year Corinne attended a basketball camp at Baylor University and lost some weight, she grew a few inches and was starting to be more confident in her appearance and abilities. This made the viciousness of their comments and jealousy increase.

They started a campaign against Corinne after she had been selected from over 500 contestants to sing in a karaoke contest in Waco, Texas. Corinne was so happy about it and proud of herself. They started again with saying she was fat, ugly, her hair was frizzy and she couldn't sing.

## A Tragic Theme

It came to a head on October 6th, 2004. That morning in PE one of the girls slapped her and called her a whore. Then the girl wrote her notes all day telling her that she was fat, ugly, had ratty hair and they wished she was dead and that she should just go home and kill herself. These girls decided that this was the "Theme of the Day" that Corinne should go home and kill herself. I knew my daughter very well; she was a very loving, sensitive person. I can only imagine the hurt and confusion my daughter was feeling that day. These girls were supposed to be her best friends and they wanted her dead. At one point Corinne wrote on her desk in one of her classes, "This school hates me," over and over again. I have been told that she had her head down and cried all day. Just as Corinne left from school that day, these girls said it again.

School let out early that day for conferences; her brothers picked her up as they always did. Corinne asked them to drive by one of these girls so she could say something to her. Her brother told her no, they needed to get home. Her brother Richard left for work at 2:00 P.M. Her brother Ronald says that she was drawing devil horns on all of one of her friend's pictures and running up and down the stairs from my room the entire afternoon. Later we found out that she had been trying to find a gun.

Ronald left for work just before 4:00 P.M., and I was home by 4:45, where I found her dead from a single gunshot to her forehead.

## Immeasurable Pain

Corinne left no note, which makes me believe she did not want to die. She just wanted a break from the pressure and to show those girls how badly they were hurting her. Her father and I believe that Corinne really thought she would just get hurt and spend some time in the hospital and [that] would fix it all, which did not happen. Instead of listening to our daughter perform at the rodeo, her father and I buried her.

The pain of losing our daughter is immeasurable. My husband wrote in her eulogy that they say you don't know what you have until it is gone, but we knew, we knew Corinne was an amazingly beautiful, talented and loving person that made every day spent with her a better day. Her family lost everything on October 6, 2004, and the world has lost more than they will ever know.

# From Bullied to Bully

## Rachel Simmons

*One prevailing theory about bullying is that bullies act out toward other vulnerable children as a defense mechanism to avoid being bullied themselves. The author of this essay would certainly agree, and has the personal experience to back it up. After suffering extreme bullying at her private middle school and high school, the author transferred to a new school, where instead of being the victim, she immediately became the aggressor.*

*Initially, she enjoyed the popularity and power that bullying gave her, but after one dramatic encounter, she made a complete shift in her life, consciously turning her back on bullies and forcing herself to change her own habits. In the process, she found, for the first time, true friends.*

*This essay originally appeared in* Odd Girl Speaks Out, *a collection of first-person accounts of girls' experiences with cliques, popularity, bullies, and jealousy.*

People think it is something one "gets over," but believe me, it's not. I was bullied in junior high and it is an experience that still affects the person I am today. It is something that will always be a part of me and something I will never forget. I really don't think I could ever forgive those girls that made my life miserable.

I was bullied, and then became the aggressor later on in life. In junior high I attended a small, upscale, private school in the Midwest. Unlike larger public schools, we had small classes of about twenty or so people. Few new kids came to our school and few kids left. It was always the same kids in the same classes, all of us together, and I believe this was a recipe for trouble.

I wasn't like the other girls. I was tall, thicker than most of the other girls. My family didn't have very much money, while the other girls came from wealthy families. My relationships with the girls were very hot and cold. One minute we were all the best of friends, but at any moment, the girls would turn on someone, usually me, and I would be completely alone.

## Continual Betrayal

Being in such a small school, when one girl hated you, all of the girls hated you, and most of the boys went along with it. And it wasn't just the grade I was in that hated me; the grades both above and below me would despise me as well. More often than not, I wouldn't even know why the girls were angry with me. But sometimes it would be a complete betrayal.

I would say something to one of the girls, usually the one I was closest to at the time. I would say something to her in confidence, and because she wanted to be popular, she would run to another girl, stab me in the back, and tell that other girl what I had said.

The result was a snowball effect, until finally what I had said had been changed so much. One time, I was so upset and so tired of being bullied and ignored that I called my grandmother and asked her to pick me up from school. I just couldn't handle it anymore. I was sick of being alone. I was sick of eating lunch by myself. I was sick of fighting back tears and I was sick of being told by teachers to just ignore the other girls. They made it sound so easy, but how can you ignore an entire class of girls calling you names?

## A New Start?

Once out of middle school I thought things would be different, but they weren't. My first year of high school, I attended an all-girls' private school. My first few months were great. I made a lot of friends and for once I felt popular and happy with who I was. But I made one false move, and everything changed for me.

I began dating a guy another girl had a crush on. I barely knew the girl and had no idea she had feelings for this boy. When I broke up with him, she started vicious rumors about me and somehow managed to "steal" all of my friends from me. It was slowly at first, a few calls not returned, a few dirty looks. But within a few weeks it escalated into a full-blown showdown during lunch. All thirteen girls ganged up on me at our lunch table, accusing me of saying things I had never said. They called me everything from a liar to a slut.

Soon, I had no friends. I sat alone at lunch. I skipped classes just so I didn't have to face any of those girls and the looks they would give me. My grades dropped dramatically. Finally, I made the decision to transfer to a public school to escape the girls and the torment. I found solace in the fact that I would be going to a new school where I knew no one. It was a chance to start over. I vowed to make a change. I did make a change, but not for the better.

## Becoming the Bully

At my new high school, I became the bully. I talked badly about girls behind their backs. I even made a few girls cry in the hallways before classes. I prided myself on being popular and in charge. No one messed with me because they knew if they did I could turn everyone that "mattered" in the school against them in no time. I was downright cruel.

For me, it was a defense mechanism. I thought if I pretended to be strong, and if I picked on everyone else that was weaker than me, no one would see the chubby girl that was tortured just years earlier. I felt as long as I was making fun of someone else, they couldn't turn the tables and make fun of me. I had the "better-them-than-me" mentality.

## A Face from the Past

It wasn't until my senior year in high school that I realized exactly what I was doing. While at the mall one evening I ran into a girl that had gone to my high school my sophomore year. I recognized her face but couldn't quite remember her name. She was tall, thin, and very pretty, so I assumed I must have been friends with her, considering my elitist and shallow attitude.

I approached her, said hello, and began making small talk. She had a look of sheer terror on her face as I talked to her.

Finally she spoke up and said, "You have no idea who I am, do you?"

I confessed that I recognized her face but couldn't remember her name.

"I'm Monica Taylor," she replied, and I knew why she had a look of disgust and horror on her face.

I had made Monica's life miserable for an entire year. I had convinced boys to make mooing sounds when she walked past them in the hallway. I laughed as my friends sat back and threw food at her during lunch. I called her everything from pig to fat and laughed as I did it. I was awful to this girl.

I was absolutely speechless and felt complete remorse when she started to cry and told me that she had had to move away because I had made her life so miserable. She revealed that her weight loss was due to an eating disorder that I directly contributed to by making fun of her weight. Her final words to me were, "You are a nasty person."

With that she walked away, and I was left with the horrible realization that I had become the very type of person I hated. I was my own worst nightmare.

## Making a Change

From that point on, I vowed to be a different person. I promised myself I would no longer make fun of people, for any reason. I couldn't make people feel as badly as people had made me feel in the past. I didn't have that right.

Making the change wasn't easy. The habit of ridiculing others was almost second nature to me. I was forced to cut ties with most of my so-called friends. I refused to spend time with people that picked on others. It resulted in a lot of backlash for me, but I came to understand that people like that weren't worth my time or effort in the first place. I knew from experience that their hurtful words stemmed from their own insecurities, not mine.

I made a real effort to get to know people I wouldn't normally spend time with and found out how wonderful those people were. I made so many real friends. I knew these people wouldn't stab me in the back or talk bad about me when I wasn't around.

I apologized to everyone I had made fun of. This was the most difficult task for me. It meant I had to admit I was wrong. It meant I had to admit that they were bigger, better people than I was. But I knew it had to be done, not just for my own sanity, but because I knew I would feel so much better if those girls who had tortured me would only apologize.

My senior year, my year of change, was one of the best of my life. I made so many new friends and found out that you don't have to be mean and hurtful to have good friends. I was more popular being respectful and kind to others than I would have ever been had I stuck with being mean.

Those experiences have made all the difference in my life, and I am grateful that I was able to see the light and make a change for the better. I hope others can see the errors of their ways and do the same someday.

# Why I Used to Be a Bully

*Angus Watson*

*Angus Watson's essay was written in response to a British government public-service campaign to reduce school bullying, similar to many programs that have been introduced in the United States. According to Watson, however, these programs—many of which urge bullied students to stand up and seek help from adults—actually promote the aura of victimization that eggs bullies on in the first place.*

*Watson should know. He was, after all, a bully during his preteen years. Despite feeling remorse for his actions toward one particular boy, Watson views most of his behavior as part of a childhood culture of violence toward oneself and others, where unkind and painful actions were seen as comedy rather than cruelty. As a former bully, Watson advocates targeting bullies—not victims—in antibullying campaigns, changing this culture of cruelty into one of kindness.*

*Angus Watson is a London-based journalist. His articles on history, travel, humor, and health have appeared in newspapers such as the* Guardian, Times of London, Financial Times, *and* Daily Telegraph.

From the ages of nine to 11, I was a bully. Anyone in my year or below who looked different, sounded funny, smelt odd or acted differently from the rest of us was fair game for physical and mental attacks. If I wasn't the main bully, I was certainly a ringleader.

Bullying tactics ranged from the psychological—constantly reminding somebody that they were fat, smelly, foreign or gay, or all four, to physical—pricking them with compasses, head-butting them, or giving them dead arms.

There was one boy, Edmund Jones, who had giant ears, yellow skin, smelt of urine and whose father was the mild-mannered French teacher. Unfortunately, because of this cruel combination of circumstances, he got it.

## A Lesson in Cruelty

One day, Bill Davis, my impressive friend from the year above, came into our classroom. There were three of us there, and Jones.

"What are you doing?" Davis asked.

"We're trying to make Jones cry just by teasing him," I answered.

"That's not how to make Jones cry," he replied, picking up Jones's cheap, heavy briefcase. He ran around all the desks gathering speed and stopped just before Jones and let go of the case. It hit Jones in the midriff like a battering ram and burst open in an explosion of paper, books, conkers [horse chestnuts] and sweet wrappers.

"That's how you make Jones cry," said Davis as Jones ran from the room sobbing.

I was awed by Davis's style and inventiveness. From that day, I raised my game. Bullying took on a crueller and more imaginative twist. Breaking expensive Caran d'Ache pencils while their owners watched, teasing them about their mothers' hairstyles, throwing sticks dipped in sheep-poo at them, and so on. Pretty horrible stuff, and certainly nothing to remember with pride. So why did I do it?

## A Culture of Pain

Other than the fact that I was plain nasty, it was part of my childhood culture. My big brother whacked me with happy regularity, as did all my dormitory captains at boarding school. One particular prefect would make us drink water until we were sick. Another made my friend cut me with an army tin opener.

My friends and I used to stab each other, and ourselves, with compasses for amusement. We used to spray deodorant from very close on to our skin, making it blister. I still have scars from that. Pain was all around. Bullying, I suppose, was a way of passing this on to the weaker boys.

I stopped when I was 12, I think, because I met girls. My parents bought a holiday house in the Isle of Wight with another family. They had twin daughters my age. My attempts to impress them and their friends by hurting smaller people were pathetic and they told me as much. So I stopped being a bully. At least, looking back, it seems that's what did it. Maybe I just grew up.

Do I feel remorse? Not really. Well, maybe a smidgen. It sounds cliched, but I feel the people I bullied grew up tougher, and more determined to prove themselves. Also, I was a completely different person then. Children are animalistic and I was running with the pack. I just happened to be one of the top dogs because of my size and knack of knowing what to say to upset people.

## Don't Be a Victim

As a reformed bully, I watch the government's "Don't suffer in silence" campaign against bullying with interest. The television advert shows that if you're a child being bullied it makes you sad, and that you should not "suffer in silence".

Part of the enterprise is a "Charter for Action". This is, for the most part, a pointlessly philosophical list of ideas for schools. For example it suggests that a school consider whether it asks itself what makes an antibullying school?

The "Don't suffer in silence" website contains an extraordinarily patronising 66-page document on how to deal with bullying. It helpfully explains that some children behave in ways that may irritate others, for example.

The central message that can be picked from the chaff of the campaign is encouragement for bullied children to tell teachers and parents. From my experience, this will only make the victim even more unpopular with everyone.

The word "victim" is key: if you "suffer in silence", then pluck up the courage to go to a teacher or parent, you are painted as a victim. The mournful youngsters in the television advert enhance this idea. Unfortunately, it is people who seem like victims who attract the unwelcome interest of the strong and cruel.

## Making Kind Cool

If the bullying is particularly serious, then of course parents and teachers need to be told. In the vast majority of cases though, the last thing someone who is being bullied needs is to be ostracised further after sneaking on their peers. Rather, the bullied want to be accepted by the people bullying them. The way to achieve this is to target the bullies, not the bullied.

A poster and television campaign saying that if you bully people you're a stupid loser, endorsed by Busted, Blazin' Squad and Britney [British and American musicians] would have a serious impact. If they could make it cool to be kind, then the likes of Edmund Jones—about whom I really do feel quite guilty—would have a much easier ride through childhood.

# CHAPTER 2

# Bullying Beyond the Basics

# Bullying in Medicine

## *Anonymous*

*Certain professions, by virtue of their high-achieving practitioners and their competitive environments, seem to lend themselves to belittling, cutthroat, or downright bullying behavior. The anonymous author of this selection writes from experience, and feels that medicine is definitely one of those professions. The author's supervisor's constant accusations of being blind, stupid, and incompetent actually caused this budding surgeon to quit practicing for a while.*

*The author's story of "learned helplessness" in the face of a bullying boss—who held hopeful physicians' futures in her hand—raises questions about how, and why, adults, especially those who have proven themselves to be competent, successful professionals, allow themselves to be bullied. It also opens up discussions about why bullying seems so intrinsic to fields like medicine, law, finance, and so forth. In particular, as the author notes, it seems ironic that medicine, "the caring profession," should lend itself to such an uncaring, even cruel, environment.*

The tears ran down my face, hidden by my surgical mask. My consultant continued relentlessly, "Why can't you do this? It really isn't hard. Are you stupid? Can't you see how to help me?"

I hated myself for crying. I avoided her eyes so she couldn't see my tears and the deep hurt in my eyes, but I couldn't speak without betraying myself. I managed a few one-word answers. The criticism continued, if not with words, then with sighs and angry tutting.

The atmosphere in the operating theatre was tense. The staff had all seen this happen many times before—hard-working, pleasant trainees reduced to nonfunctioning wrecks in the space of an operation. I looked helplessly at the scrub nurse, another trainee. She saw my distress immediately and gave me a supporting glance. But she too was suffering. "No, not that one. Why do we have to have trainees in my operations? Not like that," she lashed out at the scrub nurse. Another hard-working, competent trainee, now shaking and anxious, her self-confidence fast diminishing.

## Bad Behavior

I didn't know what to do. I felt uncomfortable continuing in such distress. Either my consultant didn't notice or she didn't care. I wondered what would happen if I asked to leave and decided that it would probably just make things worse for me. I stayed. Three hours of hostility and criticism. At the end I ripped off my mask and gloves and turned, only to have her standing behind me. She registered my swollen eyes and tear-stained face complete silence. I have never seen such a cold, emotionless stare, and I hope never to again.

Her behaviour was always the same—on the ward rounds, in clinics, and in theatre [operating room]. She was hostile, critical, and discouraging. I continued in this post for the complete six months, becoming increasingly anxious and depressed. I left my post feeling suicidal.

I am now taking a year away from medicine. The past year has been hard, coming to terms with what happened to me in my last post. I had naively hoped that bullying stopped at school. Now I know that bullies continue to bully people throughout their lives. The bullying I endured has left me traumatised. Despite being told that she treated everyone this way, I believed it was all my fault.

I couldn't believe that such an intelligent and talented surgeon should need to make herself feel better by making those around her feel terrible. I couldn't believe that this was the basis of basic surgical training. This behaviour is often seen as traditional in surgery, and when I brought it to the notice of consultants at my routine assessment and to the postgraduate dean it was ignored: further abuses of power.

## Almost Like Torture

As I look back on this time, I wonder why I felt so helpless. While trying to come to terms with the fact that I effectively let myself be bullied, I read about the experiments in which learnt helplessness was described. A dog was put in a cage and given electric shocks through one side of the floor of the cage. The dog quickly learnt to stay on the other side. The same happened when the other side was used, the dog avoiding the shocks. Then the dog received shocks from all parts of the floor at random. Initially, the dog tried to avoid them, but when unable to it gave up and lay down and received the shocks. After this the cage door was opened. The dog did not escape but stayed on the floor of the cage receiving shocks. I realised that the feeling of being unable to escape is all part of the torture.

## A Profession of Caring?

I don't know why bullying is still a part of medical training. It does not encourage learning and certainly does not bring out the best in the members of a team. In the past I have been cared for by kind and encouraging seniors. I am now a disillusioned junior doctor, not only because I was bullied by my consultant but also because she is considered suitable to train junior surgeons and because evidence of her bullying is ignored by those who should help and protect junior doctors from such inappropriate behaviour.

Perhaps some doctors should ask themselves whether they are part of the caring profession at all.

# Conversations with an Adult Bully

*Mark Goulston*

*Although it's true that, for some bullies, middle school or high school popularity is the high point of their lives, others go on to have very successful professional careers—sometimes by using the very same aggressive, belittling tactics that worked so well in their youth. In this essay, Mark Goulston describes his gradual rehabilitation of one such adult bully.*

*"Frank," who starts off their interaction by insulting a waitress, is a successful businessman and CEO. The bullying techniques that have worked well professionally, however, have been a disaster in his personal life, resulting in divorce and a painful relationship with his son. Through a series of conversations, Goulston—who may be one of the first people to dare to stand up to Frank's aggressive personality—encourages Frank to examine his own history and current behavior and to change how he interacts with others.*

*Mark Goulston is a psychiatrist and executive coach who works with individuals and corporations to improve interpersonal communication and understanding. He is the author of many articles and several books, including* Get Out of Your Own Way *and* Get Out of Your Own Way at Work.

> "The world is a dangerous place, not because of the people who are evil, but because of the people who won't do anything about it."
>
> —*Albert Einstein*

Deep within the heart of many men is the fear that they lack courage—and that they wouldn't step in the way of a bullet meant for their wife or children. They hope they will,

Mark Goulston, "My Dinner with a Bully," *Fast Company*, August 2004. Reproduced by permission.

but they aren't sure. They aren't confident. And it bothers them because a man who lacks courage isn't a man.

Many men feel this way. I have felt this way. After my first child was born, I attempted to change this. I'm still a work in progress.

## Straight Talk

"The one thing I am most happy about right now is that I don't work for you," I said emphatically.

"What?" replied my dinner appointment in surprise. Let's call this 43-year-old CEO of a rapidly growing company Frank. We had just met. And Frank had just made a condescending, sexually demeaning comment to our waitress at the famed Polo Lounge of the Beverly Hills Hotel. Our waitress could only smile back at him uncomfortably and then glance at me, as if to ask, "Who's your creepy friend?" Frank's arrogance clearly exceeded his considerable smartness. And his action pushed me to keep a commitment I'd made to myself after receiving life-saving surgery: the commitment to not allow such people into my life.

"Yeah, I wouldn't want to work for you because I would be deathly afraid to tell you if I made a mistake and because you have a capacity for contempt that crosses over into abuse," I said. "When my undiscovered mistake causes you to have to explain a mess to the board of directors, what are you going to do, blame it on a little person like me? I don't think so. After all, the company is your responsibility, isn't it? Life is just too short to put up with crap from a bully like you."

His jaw dropped. Looking at me incredulously, he said, "Nobody has ever talked to me that way."

"Well, maybe it takes one to know one," I said. "But more importantly, is it true?"

"It's all true. It cost me a marriage, a relationship with my kids, and a job," Frank confessed. Then he leaned forward and, as if he didn't want anyone to hear, and whispered, "Is it curable?"

## "It's an Addiction"

I replied without missing a beat. "It's an addiction; the best you can be is a bully in recovery," I said. "You have to work on it every day or else you'll slide back. But it's probably worth it, because at the end of your life you'll be less bitter and have more friends, and people won't have to lie at your funeral to come up with nice things to say about you. You'll accomplish more than you thought possible."

He laughed. "Can you help me?"

I pondered that for a moment. "I'm trying to figure out whether you're a bully to your core. If you delight in beating up on people, especially those who can't fight back like our waitress here, then I won't help you," I said. "That's because you have already taken from life more than you deserve. And furthermore, I would help anyone who has to deal with you to beat you. If, however, you act like a bully because it gets things done and you don't know any better, then there is some wiggle room. I might work with you."

## Time for a Change

"Which one am I?" he asked.

"Well, if I'm going to be your shrink—your coach—I get to ask the questions. Which one do you think you are?"

"I am very driven and goal oriented. I was on my cell phone after an angioplasty seven months ago," Frank explained. "But I don't think the bully bit works for me anymore, so maybe it's time for a change."

"Right answer, wrong reason," I replied, "You should change because it is wrong to abuse people, especially those below you—not because it doesn't work tactically anymore. But you have earned the right to my meeting with you once more after this dinner. You're on probation."

"Done," Frank agreed emphatically. "How soon can we start?"

## Starting on the Wrong Foot

We met the next week. I was not optimistic. I expected him to show up but not really be committed to changing. To check that out, the first thing I asked when he sat down in my office was: "What did you learn from our dinner?"

"That I may or may not be a bully," he answered, trying to be the dutiful, cooperative client.

"Close, but still wrong," I said. "You're so smart everywhere else, it's tough to figure why you're so dense here. We both know that you are very much a bully, we just don't know whether you want to change."

"Geez, you don't give a guy a break, do you?"

"Sound like anyone you know?"

"This is where you're screwed up!" he blasted back, showing his true colors. "I give everyone a chance, but when they mess up and then worse, try to cover it up, that's when I go off on them. You're being the jerk now. I should have known better than waste my time with a shrink. I've spent tens of thousands on you useless guys sending my wife and loser kids to you. And they're still not any better."

"You're right. Being glib like that was inappropriate and wrong. I'm sorry," I replied contritely.

"Too late. I must have had too many drinks at the Polo Lounge when I thought you could help me."

"I might have had one too many myself to think I could help you," I pushed back.

# Regret vs. Remorse

"Oh, screw it. I made the time on my calendar for this. Let's just move on and do it," he said in a self-serving semblance of graciousness.

"Not yet. I made an accidental glib remark, probably because I was having performance anxiety about seeing you, and then you reamed me verbally," I asserted. "That was a bit of overkill, I'd say, so I think you now owe me an apology."

"I said, 'Let's just move on,' didn't I?"

"You certainly did. Here's your lesson for today: You do regret, but you don't do remorse," I said. "You need to work on that."

"What's the difference?" he asked.

"Regret is where you admit wrongdoing and say, 'It won't happen again' and then say, 'Can't we just move on?' like you just said to me. Remorse is where you look deeply into the eyes of the person you beat up, see the damage you did, let them see that you accept responsibility for it, and then say, 'I did that. I was wrong. I'm sorry.' No excuses, no explanations, no defenses."

"Oh," he responded, a quick study even when exploring brand-new territory.

# Making Amends

I felt a little more optimistic before Frank came in the following week, but I still wasn't convinced he wanted to change. When he arrived for the next meeting, he seemed more enthusiastic. "What have you learned and done so far?" I asked.

"I've learned how much of a bully I've been, how much I need to change, and how much I want to change. I've also learned that I didn't know the difference between regret and remorse, but I do now," he responded mournfully, but happily.

"What happened?" I asked.

"I met with my 20-year-old drug-using, in-and-out-of-rehab, college-dropout son and told him I was sorry and wrong for going off on him for everything he did wrong. I told him I was sorry and wrong for almost never saying anything positive to him for what he did right—and for driving him to the point of not caring anymore," Frank admitted, his eyes watering.

"What did your son say?" I asked.

Frank's eyes reddened with tears. "He looked at me and started to cry. Then he said, barely audible, 'I'm sorry for all the times I wished you were dead and all the times I tried to kill myself because I didn't see any way out.' I asked him why he didn't tell me it was so horrible. My son looked straight through me and said, 'You didn't want to know.' You know, he was right."

"You're incredibly goal and task oriented and tune out anything or anyone that gets in the way," I said. "That's why you're so successful at work and such a failure at life—and why you're seeing me. Isn't that true?"

"You're right," he said pulling himself together.

"Here's your lesson for today: To reach goals, you have to keep control; to reach people, you have to give it up. See you next week."

When you're dealing with a person who won't do the right thing, words alone rarely have an impact. Doing the wrong thing is an action, not a statement. In the story above, it became rapidly clear that Frank wouldn't have listened to words. It was only when I threatened not to see him (something he was smart enough to know he needed) if he turned out to be a bully through and through that he really took notice.

# Teachers Can Be Bullied, Too

*Anonymous*

*For students who are bullying victims, every day at school can feel like torture. As the author of the following essay relates, however, school can seem like a trial for teachers as well—at least if those teachers are the victims of institutional workplace bullying.*

*The anonymous author of this essay did not label his workplace misery as bullying until after he had already sought help for the depression caused by his unhappiness at his job. After more than twenty years as a successful, popular high school humanities teacher, he suddenly found himself passed over for promotions, removed from a permanent office, even assigned to instruct in subjects he was not qualified to teach. His repeated inquiries and complaints seemed to fall on deaf ears. Only with the help of a psychiatrist, counselor, and physician did the author finally name the source of his problem and achieve recovery. His story illustrates that bullying can be deeply damaging, even for adults.*

I have been the victim of a school bully. But in my case the social inadequate who bullied me was my headteacher. And only after a mental breakdown, medical treatment and extensive counselling have I fully realised what happened.

My problems began in 1991 when, because of falling rolls, the school where I was a senior teacher was amalgamated [combined] with one nearby. The amalgamated school was sited in the buildings of the other school and the head of that school was appointed head of the new one.

He drew up his plans and the long process of staffing began. Most people, including myself, began planning optimistically for the future. For all my career I had worked in humanities, and in the new school everyone expected I would make an excellent leader of that faculty. Until a female PE teacher was appointed to the post.

## Back to Square One

The local education community was surprised ... and I received no counselling about my non-selection. I was eventually offered a job as an assistant teacher within the humanities area. After well over 20 years, I was going right back to where I'd started.

Over a couple of years, three senior teacher posts became available and I applied for each one. I never even reached the interview stage. It was only then that I began to think something sinister was at work.

My worries were compounded when, in my third year at the new school, I was told I would have no permanent teaching base. My world became a cheap plastic box crammed with bits and pieces—books, chalk, pens and pencils. I was the only teacher among almost 40 in this situation. I ended up teaching more subjects in more classrooms than any other member of staff. I began to feel victimised—even abused and violated. My self-esteem plummeted and confidence in my own ability hit zero.

## Getting Nowhere

In 1995, I was thrown a lifeline. The local FE [further education] college had just started a community radio project and I was seconded [allowed to transfer] to it. As the project drew to a successful end, I looked for work away from the school environment. But my age (late forties) conspired against me. When the project ended in 1997, there was no alternative for me but to return to the school where I had been so unhappy and seemingly so unwanted.

While I'd been away the school had appointed three more senior teachers. The head had not notified me about any of these vacancies, all of which would have been well suited to my experience and background. This new management team had also made significant changes to the school structure, one of which was deciding that new intake pupils would be taught as if they were still in primary school—they would have the same teacher in the same room for most of their school week. I was to be one of those "new style" teachers. After almost 25 years of secondary school specialist teaching, I was being asked to work like a general subject primary teacher. Training? Guidance? Support? Nothing was provided.

The career structure I had aspired to was in tatters. My discussions with the head met with the same shrugged shoulders of earlier years. My difficulties seemed to him at best trivial. I tried hard to succeed but was getting nowhere. I instinctively knew the quality of my lessons was deteriorating. This was not the way to end my career. After a lifetime of quality teaching, I was back to being an assistant teacher, trying to deliver subjects about which I knew very little. The classroom became a mental jail and I could see no escape.

## Battling Depression

The black dog of depression that had yapped at my heels a couple of years earlier was now biting hard. I entered a downward spiral of stress and deepening depression. I began to drink heavily and to distance myself from my family. I was withdrawn and had no energy. My life was drifting away from me. During odd constructive moments, I applied for other jobs, both in and out of education. But the growing list of rejections only accelerated my depression and feeling of severe, self-inflicted failure.

In the depth of my depression I left home, with no good reason other than to be alone, and away from the very people who were willing to help me. The blackness intensified. Dark nights and darker days.

Then I was rescued by the woman on whom I had inflicted so much pain during my sullen descent. My wife took me back and urged me to visit a doctor and within days I was starting a long, slow and often painful recovery. My doctor was sympathetic and highlighted the problems immediately: my job, the school, and the treatment meted out to me there. He immediately gave me a sick note and arranged professional counselling.

## A Final Chance

I decided to give the school one last chance. I rang to make an appointment to talk to the head and turned up with a half-rehearsed plea for time and compromise. His secretary made me wait in a busy corridor. I felt invisible. Old colleagues passed me by without a word, pupils hurried on and seemed to sneer at me. I felt an acute sense of panic. I was exposed and vulnerable.

The head arrived 20 minutes late and ushered me into his office. The tiny amount of confidence I'd summoned had vanished. He was dominant and frightening. Why had I expected anything different? Some single moments in your life can crystallise circumstances, and this was such a moment. I left and have never seen him again.

The day after, I began a course of individual counselling, and also visited Relate [a family counseling program] with my wife for guidance about our relationship, which was now growing in understanding.

## Naming the Problem

My counsellor broached the subject of bullying in the workplace and over the course of our meetings we explored the problem. It was clear to her that bullying was at the root of my depression. She also suggested psychiatric help, and again the consultant was clear that bullying was central to my problem. He prescribed strong drugs to help me through this cathartic [healing] period. My doctor, counsellor and psychiatrist were adamant that I would never return to teaching. I didn't argue.

Having acknowledged the problem and with a clear support structure, I was growing stronger by the day. But anger was never far away. Anger at the way I'd been treated, but also at myself for allowing events to run me.

At times a guilt replaced the anger, and the depression would blacken. But with time the outbursts of anger and guilt became fewer and fewer. During this long period the school made no contact. This only underlined what I was slowly realising: I had been the victim of an abusive school bully. His power was such that even now, by his inaction, he was exerting control over me.

After six months absence the LEA [Local Education Authority] was legally obliged to contact me. I saw their doctor, and they suggested I take early retirement on grounds of ill health. I accepted and retired. My teaching career was over.

## Going Back

At last the school contacted me—a letter from the head. The note was five sentences long. After almost 30 years, I merited five brief sentences. He stayed a bully right to the end.

Shortly after I retired I went back to the school.

As I got out of the car, an old colleague saw me and stopped. At last, I thought, I was to be acknowledged. He looked through me and beyond. Then he slowly turned his back. That gesture said everything. For whatever reason, I no longer existed and that really hurt. Contact with me, it seemed, meant failure.

Or perhaps my colleagues saw in my bully-induced depression a vision of what might happen to them. Maybe, by hiding their heads in the sand and pretending I do not exist they think they can also avoid the problem. I know with certainty that they are wrong.

# Mean Girls Never Grow Up

*Victoria A. Brownworth*

*As Victoria A. Brownworth notes in her essay, the phenomenon of female bullying has been exposed in recent years, with books like* Queen Bees and Wannabes *and* Odd Girl Out, *and films like* Mean Girls. *Brownworth's story illustrates, however, that this culture of female aggression (which often takes the form of gossip, backstabbing, and exclusion) is still alive and well, even in communities of adult women.*

*Brownworth thought her teenage years of enduring bullying were well behind her when she was forced to confront a new community of bullies—a clique of particularly nasty women who staged a cyberbullying campaign against Brownworth in an on-line "support" community for lesbians. Online rumor-mongering and exclusion are difficult enough for mature women to cope with—how, Brownworth questions, are still-maturing, vulnerable teens supposed to handle them?*

*Victoria A. Brownworth is a nationally syndicated columnist, writing book reviews for the* Baltimore Sun *and a regular column for* Curve *magazine. She has written numerous books, including* Coming Out of Cancer: Writings from the Lesbian Cancer Epidemic.

I was bullied at school. Mercilessly. Before *Heathers* and the "Plastics," before books and studies about girls who bully, before it was a recognizable trend, there was me, isolated and alone in my all-girls Catholic school, bullied every day.

The reasons why I was bullied are numerous. I was a smart girl, and intellectual geeks are always targets. I was also the tallest girl in my class, and my gawkiness was made worse by a uniform and saddle shoes.

Victoria A. Brownworth, "Mean Girls Never Grow Up: They Just Get New Screen Names," *Curve*, vol. 18, May 2008, pp. 30–31. Copyright © 2008 Curve Magazine. Reproduced by permission.

I came from a dysfunctional home, so my social skills were sketchy.

My family was poor, so I was regularly called out for unpaid tuition in front of the entire class. At events where we wore regular clothes instead of uniforms, my classmates were attired in chic little Villager and Lady Bug mini-skirts. I was wearing clothes my mother had made or things she had bought at the thrift shop. Rickrack was almost always involved.

## Echoes from the Past

If you're bullied in childhood, it can lead to a lack of self-esteem. But even if you grow up to become popular and successful, those mean-girl taunts remain in the back of your head, echoing into your adult life.

Lesbian life is full of mean girls. We've all run into them. They're in the bars, in the activist groups, on the email lists. . . . They haunt our community with their rumor-mongering and nasty asides.

My school was claustrophobically small, just like the lesbian community so often is, even in big cities like my own. There was nowhere to hide from the hierarchy of cliques.

The lesbian community can be the same way. As vast as it can appear when you first come out and don't know how to navigate the terrain, it can suddenly seem like a crowded elevator stalled between floors when you break up with someone or leave a particular group.

## Cyberbullying

A few months ago, a story made all the news outlets about a young girl who committed suicide after being bullied mercilessly online. It was a tragic story and made me think about the new trend in bullying: hit and run on the Internet, where anyone can post anything about another person, and the victim has no recourse.

Megan Meier was only 13-years-old when she hanged herself in her bedroom closet after being bullied online. The girl thought she was being bullied by a boy she met on MySpace. It turned out the "boy" was the creation of a former friend's mother and this woman was the real bully.

Mean girls never stop being mean girls, even when they grow up.

Meier's case is perhaps extreme. But many girls are bullied online and just suffer through it, afraid to tell anyone for fear the bullying will get worse.

This is the Internet Age, and everyone has a cyber life in addition to their daily offline life. Adolescence is primed for bullying, but so is the Internet.

## No Boundaries in Cyberspace

I've been involved with online groups over the years—some political, some queer. I discovered in my cyber life that mean girls never grow up—they just get new screen names.

One of the problems I had at school was that I couldn't mislead or conceal. I was only ever good at being myself. I never did develop that trait of dissembling. As a consequence, I am the same in real life as I am online.

But that's not the case for many people in cyberspace. As Meier found out all too tragically, mean girls haunt the cyber world, trolling for victims on whom to vent their prodigious spleen.

The difference between cyberspace and the real world is that in the real world you can't say or do anything you want without consequences. But online, anything goes. You can use vile language, lie about someone, invent new identities, steal others; or trash a life and just move on.

## Cliques All Over Again

I found this out firsthand when a lesbian email list I had belonged to for almost a decade let its mean girls take over. It began with an argument over politics, but then it escalated into something more sinister. I began receiving nasty offline messages from a few members of the group. These were startling and hurtful, and I requested that the harassment stop. It didn't, so I just deleted the mean girls' emails.

Then there was a shocking twist: The woman who started the group ousted me. She sent a letter to the group saying they were not "allowed" to talk to me about why she did so.

The years of bullying came back in a tsunami, knocking me flat. It was as if I were back in that schoolyard all over again. It was a terrible feeling.

## No Way Out

My story has a much happier ending than the Meier one. Many of the group's members left in solidarity with me and I started a new group, which has none of the tensions of the old one.

But for several weeks after my expulsion, I was in the tortured place of the victim with no recourse. In real life, I could have sued the list maven for the things she said about me—lie upon lie fed to her by the women who had been bullying me for months. In real life, I would have been able to face my accusers and ask for evidence and, when none was presented, been vindicated.

But the terror of online bullying is that there is no redress, no way out for the victims. And when those victims are young and resourceless, the results can be tragic.

I saw myself in Megan Meier, because I was her, many years ago. I attempted suicide as a kid; the bullying was that harrowing for me. I spent years cutting my arms with razor blades in an effort to release the pain.

Then, magically, I became an adult and life was under my control. I survived.

## Keep the Mean Girls in Check

Mean girls proliferate in all walks of life. They cut their vicious little teeth on childhood pariahs and then move on to bigger targets. Whenever I read a column by [*New York Times* journalist] Maureen Dowd on [senator] Hillary Clinton, for example, I imagine she was a mean girl pushing and shoving her way through the schoolyard.

As adult women, we often equate viciousness with strength, but they are not the same thing. Being on the receiving end of a mean girl's poisonous pen or whiplash tongue can end tragically, as it did for Megan Meier.

We need to rein in the mean girls in our own communities and never let them gain the advantage or create more victims. Mean girls give all women a bad name and can damage impressionable young girls—sometimes, as with Megan Meier, beyond repair.

# Just a Little Pro-Bullying

*Katrina Onstad*

*The starting point for Katrina Onstad's article is a* Good Morning America *interview with actress Reese Witherspoon, where she voiced the opinion that it might, sometimes, be good for kids to be bullied—at least a little. Onstad, who's also a mother, admits that she's had many of the same thoughts, particularly as she witnesses other overly protective parents swoop in and cushion their children from the bumps and bruises of everyday life in the outside world.*

*The culprit, Onstad argues, is a culture and a parenting philosophy entirely focused on building up children's self-esteem. Onstad asks a provocative question here: What if, by solving all their kids' problems for them, parents are actually robbing their children of a chance to develop their own sense of self-worth?*

*Katrina Onstad is a Canadian film critic and writer whose film reviews and criticism have appeared in* Salon.com, *the* New York Times, *and* Toronto Life. *She also writes a regular column for the Canadian magazine* Chatelaine *and is the author of the novel* How Happy to Be.

Reese: "I Want My Kids Teased and Bullied!"

The headline, which ran on a New York gossip site earlier this year, is a provocation, another celebrity outburst so outrageous that it can't possibly be true. What kind of mother wants her kids to be bullied, their self-esteem shredded? Well, I finally have something in common with Reese Witherspoon besides bangs: I think I might be a little pro-bullying, too. Just a little bullying, just a little pro.

Here's what Witherspoon actually said in the interview with *Good Morning America*: "I don't want my children to miss out on any of that teasing and bullying. It kind of makes you who you are, when you don't make it onto the soccer team. I remember the two weeks of crying because I didn't make the volleyball team. It made me interesting."

What she's talking about is vastly different from the kind of repetitive, torturous bullying that has played a part in the deaths of children and teens across the country. Nothing can, or should, diminish the horror of the kind of extreme bullying—online and in the flesh—that led a gay Grade 9 student named Shaquille Wisdom to kill himself in Ajax, Ontario, last fall [2007].

## You Cannot Always Protect Your Kids

But somewhere on the playground between sugar-and-spice and evil is the kind of quotidian meanness that our kids will face forever. Trying to protect them from every slight, every taunt, is an act of hubris, but it's not surprising that parents try: Emotional safety is the next frontier now that we've fooled ourselves into thinking we've conquered physical safety. Parents put plastic over every sharp edge, install nanny cams in daycares and play on-call chauffeur in an exhausting sprint to remove all risk and quell all panic.

But emotional safety is harder to guarantee. When my four-year-old came home from school telling me about a boy who wouldn't play with him, I didn't see any signs of damage—he reported the event in a neutral way—but then he said, "Bullies are bad." My son is a quick study, and he'd absorbed the language of victimization along with everything else: Egyptians were buried in tombs; the sea is salty; bullies are out to get me.

I called the teacher the next day, asking if I should be concerned. With extreme patience, she assured me there was no bullying going on and that the school had "zero tolerance" for it. I sensed that she gets a lot of these calls. In Toronto, where I live, the school board released a new bullying prevention and intervention policy in January and recently set up a hot-line where kids can report a number of school abuses, including bullying. I admire the intent of these initiatives, but my recollection of childhood cruelty is that bullies are like cockroaches: adaptable. If they want to call your son a loser, they will.

## Learning to Stand Up for Yourself

But is all aggression equal? Recently, a Toronto parent complained that her son was suspended from school for throwing a snowball at another student: an act of bullying. Later, after the horrific murder of 15-year-old Jordan Manners, shot in the hallway of his Toronto public high school, the school board released a panel investigation into school safety. The report stated that serious incidents of physical violence too often went unreported by students and teachers across the city. Why is our focus so off?

In his new book, *Sissy Nation*, the journalist John Strausbaugh argues that Americans are too soft, a nation of coddled and somnambulant citizens with no ability to think for themselves. Sissy, he has said, isn't about being gay or feminine: "It has to do with your brains and your commitment and your conviction and your ability to stand up as an individual"—or lack thereof.

I don't love Strausbaugh's thesis—America seems pathologically un-sissyish in its testosterone-fuelled foreign policy these days—but it strikes me as germane to how we raise our kids. When parents protect their children too intensely, we rob them of agency. A child who learns how to handle a bully is armed for life, but when an authority figure steps in, the kid learns only that he will always be saved. Figuring out how to navigate cruelty doesn't merely build character, it also rouses one to empathize with those who cannot, will not, be rescued.

## Self-Esteem . . . at What Price?

Parents call teachers and hover outside the playground gates not only because they care, but because experts tell them to get in there. For years, the dominant parenting philosophy has asserted that self-esteem is the most important attribute to instill in a kid, and to get it requires constant intervention: rewards, praising, more praising, rewards. The result, writes the parenting expert Barbara Coloroso, one of the most sensible voices in the mix, is a generation of "praise junkies." These kids are given scratch-and-sniff stickers at the first successful potty moment, then good-grade bonuses throughout school, until they arrive in the world with a shrug asking, "What's in it for me?"

Witherspoon, that truth teller, also said, "It drives me crazy when everyone wins the award." Today's parents would probably call the volleyball coach and advocate on behalf of poor, sad Reese, no matter how lousy her spike. But in fact, her self-esteem probably improved for not getting on that team. She learned that she could handle rejection and succeed at a few other things with her life, like, say, acting. The fact is, not everyone deserves a slot on the volleyball team. Our kids are precious, but mostly only to us. If they approach the world assuming the same soft landing they've had at home all their lives, they will only fall harder.

## Are We Too Proud of Ourselves?

China has recently admitted to significant labour shortages in a few key manufacturing areas. A generation of "little emperors" reared since the instigation of China's one-child policy has given way to a population of adults who feel above this station, unwilling to do the factory jobs their parents did.

Of course young people have every right to strive for better, but then what? Many of this type of Chinese youth (mostly male) are invested in their own personal success—after all, they're the centre of the universe—but how do they feel, I wonder, about those around them? How are their powers of empathy? It's a question worth asking of kids in our own backyard, too, one that may be suffering from too much self-esteem—of overestimating their worth and accomplishments.

Of course, I don't want my kids to feel pain, to be teased or hurt. But if they don't sometimes confront the depths of another person's cruelty, then they will have nothing against which to measure their own humanity. By butting out, we give them that gift.

SOCIAL ISSUES
FIRSTHAND

# CHAPTER 3

# Overcoming the Effects of Bullying

# A Survivor's Story

## Lorie A. Johnson

*Like many long-time targets of bullying, Lorie A. Johnson has spent much of her adult life recovering from the blows to her self-esteem she suffered in her youth. In Johnson's case, graduating from high school was like a deliverance from evil, as she was finally able to escape the students who had made every day of her public school career a trial.*

*In the years following graduation, Johnson underwent therapy, wrote about her experiences, and used martial arts to understand why she had failed to fight back. She also took great solace in finally understanding—with the help of a former teacher—why bullies attack out of weakness and why those who are bullied often become more interesting, more successful, and more fulfilled adults than do their tormentors. Although Johnson's story is far from positive, she does tell her history from a position of strength and understanding, finding power in her own successes and reminding readers that they have many ways to combat bullying, but their best ally is time.*

*Lorie A. Johnson is an Air Force veteran and a computer support specialist. She writes on many topics, including spirituality, paganism, Wicca, and the occult.*

I was a military brat. Military brats are unique creatures in that we have to be flexible, adaptable and able to accept change. I was able to do this, and in many ways I believe that this internal resilience helped to get me through school. I lived in many interesting places, saw and did many interesting things. I would not trade the experiences I had as a military kid for anything—except for school. School was the Dark Side of my life, the place of humiliation and torment.

Lorie A. Johnson, "Black Lightning: A Survivor's Tale," *Ravendays* (www.ravendays.org), 2001. Reproduced by permission.

I had a little hint of what was to come when I was in fifth grade. I was a brilliant and gifted student, and because of this, was the darling of my teachers, and the target of bullies. One girl in particular was my chief tormentor. For some reason, she hated everything about me—my hair, my glasses, and probably, my ease at reading in front of others. She took particular delight in getting the other girls to gang up on me and rip out handfuls of my long hair. My teacher told my mom that if I had fought back, she "wouldn't have seen a thing." I never did.

## Home Sweet Home

True hell began when my family returned to the US, and I went to off-base schools. I became the victim of my mother's fashion sense. In the early 70s, the clothing sold at the local K-Mart was stunningly hideous, and I would cry at the things my mom would get for me. Her choice of eyeglasses for me was also awful—I begged for wire-rimmed glasses, but would end up with what my mom thought looked nice on me—light blue, sixties-era cat-eyes. She would have done better to paint a target on my back when she sent me to school in the wilds of Arkansas. The abrupt silence that greeted me when I walked into the classroom was the opening overture to the five years of sheer hell that followed. I was beat up on the very first day of school. My glasses were replaced 10 times between the 7th and 9th grades, when my mom finally gave in and permitted me to have the wire-rims I so desperately wanted.

I rode my bike to sixth grade, and would often find my tires flat, the paint scratched, or the seat slashed. Someone partially cut through the gear control cable, and it broke and tangled in my front wheel when I was going full speed down a steep hill. To this day I remember the screams of derision from my classmates as they zipped by me as I lay bleeding and half-conscious in the middle of the street. A base security policeman scooped me up and took me home. My dad made me go to school that day, even though I was in obvious shock. "Why don't you tell me who did it?" he demanded many times, several in the emergency room where I was being splinted yet again. He wouldn't accept my insistence that most everyone was in on it. He thought I was lying, and I overheard many nasty arguments between my parents about what to do about me.

## Unable to Fight Back

How could I be their daughter, when I wouldn't fight? My passive acceptance of the kicks, fists, pinches and other indignities puzzled my parents. Why wouldn't I fight back? They tried to get me to take self-defense classes. Dad tried to teach me to box. Mom constantly wished she could "be in my body" for just one day, and she'd straighten out my tormentors. Boys in particular singled me out to grab my breasts, stick their hands between my legs, or snap my bra straps. I would try to get the teachers to get them to stop. "Boys will be boys," I'd hear. Or, "He likes you." (This after a particularly painful "noogie" to my head.) The ones who wore the Converse baseball shoes were particularly vicious; they were the proto-jocks who shadowed me all through junior high and some of high school. There was the cavalier attitude of the privileged about them, and the knowledge that they could—and did—get away with just about anything. I loathed them.

High school was also hell, but with the exception of an occasional grope from a steroid-addled jock, the torment became more psychological than physical. It was bad enough that I dreaded getting up in the morning, and nightly wished I would not awaken the next day. It didn't help that my father teased me constantly; my vehement dislike of the male sex was a source of gleeful teasing that would leave me in frustrated tears. He would threaten to marry me off to the first hick who asked. In Arkansas, early marriage was the norm, and it was a while before I found out that he could not do that. Still, I had nightmares about something like that happening for years after I left home.

The overtly physical torment I suffered trickled off, to be replaced by social and psychological rejection. I didn't talk, act, or dress like them, nor did I grow up with them, which automatically made me an outcast. I wasn't "saved," either, and the more religious of them would single me out for derision and Biblical bad-mouthing. I was also the target of Christian "love-bombing": intense, but false "friendships" meant to lure the lonely and the outcast into going to their churches and being converted. When I did not fall for this bait, I was ostracized even worse.

## Escape Through Books

I found an outlet in reading, and escaped through Star Trek and science fiction. Even though I was going to go straight into the USAF [United States Air Force], I still took a full load of AP [Advanced Placement] classes for the sheer fun of it. I refused to participate in the teen rituals my mom wanted me to go to—the dances, the prom, and all that. Why should I set myself up for ridicule? Around that time, *Carrie* was published, and I very strongly identified with her. I turned my back on the social whirl of the school year and lost myself in books. I was 300 books short of reading the entire library when I graduated. Computers were still very primitive, but I was geeky enough to be allowed to watch an expensive (back then) calculator get dissected. I was the only one who knew which circuits were what, and actually got an admiring comment from a guy. Too bad it was late in my senior year. But that comment was the first bit of light in the long darkness of my youth, and I eagerly soaked it up.

It was during my senior year when I had a very interesting and enlightening conversation with my school guidance counselor. He was one of those youngish, mod sorts who tried his best to be "in" with the kids, but never quite got it. He was also an early version of the New-Age hippie sort, and was interested in all sorts of esoteric things. "Did you know that you have the highest IQ in the school?" he asked me. I did not know that, nor did I know that the school wanted to skip me forward a grade, back in the sixth grade. My parents told them no. "Why aren't you going to college?" I couldn't articulate it at the time, but I was afraid that college would be socially the same as high school. The Air Force was more attractive to me. My counselor told me that I was an "old soul"— because I dealt with the slights and head-games of my peers in a very dignified and mature manner. He foresaw a good life ahead for me. I told him that all I saw was that diploma in my hand, and the school marquee in the rear view mirror— that was my mental goal.

## A Fresh Start

The day I graduated in 1979 was the day that I truly began to live. It took many years for me to heal the scars inflicted upon my soul by my tormentors, and to gain the grizzled self-confidence that today is my stock in trade. I daily believe that the later part of my life will be (and is rapidly becoming) the best part. I managed to survive my childhood with my sanity intact. I battled severe depression in my twenties and early thirties, but conquered that, too. I worked in computer retail for several years after my military career ended, and learned the art of graciously shutting down bullying men who thought they knew more about computers and electronics than I did. My motto became: "Do Not Mess with the little blonde TechMage, for you are stupid and make a great target!"

In retrospect, I know why I didn't fight back. I was afraid— afraid not of hitting my tormentors, but afraid that if I started, I would not be able to stop until I had killed them. My martial arts instructor helped me to uncover this, and turn this black and overpowering rage into an awesome weapon that I can control. He called it the "Black Lightning," and told me that it is the source of the so-called "death touch" in some martial-arts forms. I told him about my school days and my fears. He looked me in the eye and told me that I was right to fear this power, because it was there even when I was a child. I had to stay away from practice for a few weeks while this understanding found its place within me. I left the class several months later for unrelated reasons.

## Coming Full Circle

The telling full-circle moment came last fall, during elections. I had returned to my home state, and had settled into the same neighborhood I grew up in. Running for a county office was my former high school social studies teacher. I didn't think he'd remember me when I introduced myself, but to my surprise, he did. We had coffee together, and he told me that he had wondered what became of me. He was the only teacher who actively defended me when I was being picked on, and I remember him making a bullying jock stand in the middle of the classroom and hold two encyclopedias in an "iron cross" configuration. He told me that he knew I was different, and hoped that I would do well after I left school. I told him that I still had nightmares occasionally, but that I felt the worst part of my life was over. The man had a memory that was incredible, and related to me the fate of many of my tormentors. Two had died in an alcohol-related car crash in college. Others were in prison, or had criminal records. Several of the proud crowd girls were on their fourth husbands, and already had grandkids. Many were dead or dying, or diseased. Other of my peers were more successful. One went on to teach at the school she graduated from, another is a prominent psychologist on the west coast. Another is a coach. Most of the women had kids. I told him that I remembered him classifying the lot of us in various cliques as a part of our social studies class. Some were jocks, some were band-jocks, others were preppies or proud crowd, and there were the stoners, the greasers, the brides-to-be, and me. He couldn't classify me at all, which made for some amusement in the room. He remembered that, and told me that he figured out who I, and others like me were: mature misfits. Young adults. Geeks in the good sense. Intellectuals-in-waiting. It was gratifying to hear that from him. He went on to win his seat in the election.

## In Retrospect

Today, at 40, I am successful in my job, confident in myself, and know in my deepest marrow that no one can ever hurt me the way I was hurt as a youth. I am an accomplished occultist, respected writer, and sought-after speaker on technical subjects. I have learned about the healing side of the Black Lighting, and have done a lot of work to repair my self-esteem. I am also a keen judge of character, and can spot out a bully in a line-up of identically dressed people in a heartbeat. I bear deep scars from my torment, and even today, there is a certain type of male that totally repulses me. It took me a long time to trust men and see them as human beings, but I have never married, and do not intend to. Yet I hate no one, and hold no grudges against any of my former tormentors. Although today I could peel them like an onion, I know I will not have to. For me, my success, survival, wisdom and insight are my best revenge, and I have no need to drive the screws still farther into their debt-ridden, pot-bellied, spouse and kiddie-whipped carcasses.

There was no rhyme or reason to their torment of me, except for that animal fear of the odd one. Their hate and fear was very primitive and very basic. I now see it as doomed animals (them) turning against the proto-humans (people like me). Human animals try to harm that which they cannot understand or that which they fear. Perhaps it is the same today—with the targets being the quiet and intelligent ones who can see the social bullshit for what it really is, and the tormentors for the sheeple [unthinking followers] they really are. And the sheeple, ignorant as they are, know this, know that they are bound for eventual cultural slaughter and consumption by the life-script of school, job, marriage, debt, kids, and the SUV, and lash out with the last desperate twitch of their doomed souls. High school is the high point of many of these tormentors' lives; in their marrow they know that their lives are over after they graduate, even if they go on to college. Many try to carry on the high school mentality into college, but the gig is over by then, and no one will dance.

## The Best Revenge

I survived my childhood. It's funny to say that now, but in retrospect, that is what I did—survived, in spite of their best efforts to eliminate me.

If you, dear reader, are still in what [author] Jon Katz calls "the Hellmouth," take heart. It ends. When you leave school, you enter the adult world, where people don't beat you up because they can. If you are intelligent, articulate, mature, responsible, you will be sought after; not for torture, but for those very qualities the savages in school loathe. If you should encounter a bully, you have recourse—everything from Human Resources to lawsuits. If that bully is a superior, you can leave. You don't have to take it. It isn't your problem, it is theirs.

It will take you some time to get on your feet and get over the torment. But today, you have many more resources than I did 20 years ago. Use them. Get counseling if you need to. Get your depression treated. Turn the page, and know that your own best years are ahead of you—even as your tormentors' best years are behind them.

And never, ever forget: Success is the best revenge.

# Finding Self-Acceptance

*Jason Shen*

*Frequently, those who are targets of bullying feel isolated and alone. Reaching out to others is an effective way to combat those feelings of loneliness and vulnerability, whether by finding support online or by joining a supportive, nonbullying group at school, at church, or in the community. That was certainly Jason Shen's experience, as he shares in this essay.*

*Tired of enduring taunts about his appearance and the resulting feelings of inadequacy around girls, Shen decided to join his school's mock trial team. Although he was soon subjected to a different kind of bullying (from the lawyers who served as the team's coaches), he also discovered, through his hard work and success, the self-confidence and pride he had always lacked.*

*Shen's essay won first place in the Kaplan/Newsweek My Turn Essay Competition. After high school, he went on to be a regents scholar at the University of California, Los Angeles, majoring in psychobiology with the goal of attending medical school.*

I can't remember the first time the bullies called me Kermit. Or Froggy. Or Toad. It has become such an integral part of me that I can't imagine myself without the nicknames.

It's not easy being ugly. OK, not ugly. That's too harsh. Not facially endowed. What else can you call a guy who resembles an amphibian? People say you shouldn't judge a book by its cover, but among teenagers, the cover is what sells the book. I watched from the sidelines as my more attractive friends matched up and broke up without a care. For me, one glance from a girl was enough to feed my heart, which was shrunken from deprivation like a hunger-stricken stomach. I'd lie in my room, listen to Sister Hazel's "Change Your Mind" and swear it was about me: "If you wanna be somebody else. . . ."

## A New Outlet

At the beginning of my senior year of high school, I joined the mock-trial team. I needed a better way to spend my time than idling in front of my computer trying not to think of what my best friend was doing on his date with his girlfriend.

At the tryouts, in order to gauge my speaking skills, one of the lawyers who would coach the team looked me in the face and asked, "What do you think of the HIV epidemic in Africa?" Somehow, I stammered out a comprehensible answer. Surprisingly, I was awarded one of the six coveted attorney positions, while the rest of my 19 teammates were relegated to witness or clerk roles.

It was clear from the start that our training would be intense. One of the lawyer-coaches put it bluntly: "At work we charge 500 bucks an hour. We're with you guys at least 10 hours a week. You do the math. Now you want to shut up and listen?"

## Finding Confidence

At every practice, the coaches would cruelly criticize our every mistake and call us everything short of complete idiots. Our opening statements were too short, our direct examinations were too long and our cross-examinations just plain stank. Then, just before we'd break down, they'd build us back up by showing us how much we had improved. Before long, we were flexing our mental muscle like true lawyers.

After our two months of training, the first competition rolled around. Before we entered the county courtroom, one of our coaches offered us some not-so-gentle encouragement: "Winning's not everything. It's the only thing."

When I walked to the podium in my suit to stand before the real-life superior-court judge and examine the "witness," a new sensation grabbed hold of me. It took me a minute to realize that it was confidence, a feeling I had never fully experienced, definitely not while conversing with a girl or sitting alone at a party. At the end of the trial, I gave my closing argument. I forget exactly what I said that made the audience, and even the other team, stand up and applaud. I just remember smiling so much that it hurt, especially as the judge singled me out as a "silver-tongued devil."

The next month seemed the shortest of my life, as my team turned in a whirlwind of amazing performances. Before we knew it, we were in the sweet 16, the elite group that remained from the original 64 teams. Three rounds later, we advanced to the final match to determine who would go on to the state championships.

## "The Moment Was Beautiful"

The opposing team was as polished and impressive as a real dream team of lawyers. They countered all of our normally impressive arguments with even more impressive arguments of their own. As I got up to give what I thought would be my last closing statement of the year, I told myself to relish every second of it. After this, it was back to the real world, where my speaking skills were of little value to my superficial peers. I practically cried during the best closing I ever gave.

I actually did cry when, after I finished, the judge announced that my team had won and the room exploded in a roar of celebration. I hugged my co-counsels to the brink of suffocation, then rushed around congratulating the rest of my teammates. One of my coaches heartily shook my hand and admitted with a grin, "Even I was impressed."

Then I heard it. "Kermit!" I whipped around to see who had teased me. My best friend stood in front of me, beaming. To my surprise, he had come to watch me compete. "Jason," he said, "I've never heard such an articulate frog."

The team began to chant, "Silver-tongued frog! Silver-tongued frog!" In that moment I realized that I was no different from teenagers everywhere who struggle to be accepted; I won the struggle because I learned to accept myself. In that moment I was actually proud to be an amphibian. That moment was beautiful.

# The Dodgeball Wars

*Ayelet Waldman*

*Parenthood is a complicated business, especially if you're a parent who still bitterly remembers being ostracized (at best) or taunted (at worst) as a child. That's the experience of writer Ayelet Waldman, who acknowledges that being a nerd formed her character but admits that she always imagined that she—unlike her own mother—would stick up for her own children, championing them if and when they became as unpopular as she once was.*

*All that changed, though, when Waldman's two oldest children fell in love with the gym class game of dodgeball, universally loathed by wimpy, nerdy kids everywhere and still fresh in the memory of Waldman herself, who recalls gym class as the worst trial of all. Hearing their raves about dodgeball, Waldman is forced to admit that her children will live their own lives, and that her kids—who have, despite their genetic background, become popular—just might have to form their own characters in other ways.*

*Ayelet Waldman is an essayist and novelist, and author of the "Mommy-Track Mysteries" series.*

A couple of months ago, my two oldest kids came home from school abuzz over the new game they'd learned in gym class. I'd never heard them express any kind of excitement about P.E. before—they are not natural athletes—but there they were strategizing and recounting the high points of their respective matches with unprecedented zeal. I tried to follow the discussion, but it was making little sense to me. My one foray into organized sports was a single spring on the Brookwell Cleaners Softball Team in 6th grade. I remember

Ayelet Waldman, "Blast from the Past," Salon.com, June 2005. This article first appeared in Salon.com at http://www.salon.com. An online version remains in the Salon archives. Reprinted with permission.

very little about the season other than the ache in my shoulder from holding my hand above my head in a futile attempt to distract the gnats from my face, the sound of my own teammates' jeers as I made my regular strikeout, and the euphoria of being allowed to take the bench whenever our team had the slightest chance of winning.

The game my kids were so agog over wasn't softball, though. It wasn't even foursquare, a game they'd once tried to explain to me without much success. Finally, I asked them what they were talking about.

"Dodgeball!" my 7-year-old son announced, gleefully. "It's really fun."

Dodgeball? My children were playing *dodgeball?* That cruel, brutal, violent schoolyard game so mercilessly satirized in the 2004 film with Ben Stiller? The game, more important, that exemplified everything that was wrong with my childhood in suburban New Jersey, a short, pasty-faced Jewish girl in a town full of scrubbed, blond, athletic WASPs, their long tanned limbs toned from years of tennis lessons and country club swim teams? Dodgeball? Over my dead body.

## Flashback to Gym Class

I know it's fashionable to claim to have been a nerd as a child, to insist on having scrabbled to hold on to the lowest tier of the social ladder, to recount years of torture at the hands of the golden and anointed. Trust me, I know just how trite my history of exclusion is. I know that when compared to a lifetime of true deprivation and abuse, suburban misery counts for little. Nonetheless, as someone who still, at 40, gets a clutch of nausea every time she drives by George Washington Junior High School, I am just not willing to let go of the reins of this particular hobbyhorse. I am convinced that my entire personality was formed in those long tile hallways where I was a victim of that most banal of childhood torments—ostracism. Everything can be explained by, every torque and twist in my character can be attributed to, those grim, lonely years. Neither the jocks, nor the heads, not even the brains wanted any part of me. The other kids didn't talk to me, or even look at me, and if it weren't for the series of successively more hostile prank phone calls that I received, I could have happily deluded myself into thinking that none of them knew I existed.

Gym class, however, was where they allowed themselves to express their disdain. In gym class for some reason they were allowed to heap derision on the apraxic [uncoordinated] kids. ("No batter, no batter. Easy out.") Gym class was, of course, where the strongest, best-looking kids were made captains and chose us spazzes last. More important, it was where the figures of supposed authority allowed them to do so. Forget the work our parents did molding our minds and values. Everything fell apart as soon as we put on those maroon polyester gym suits.

And dodgeball. God, dodgeball. As my own children were planning their tactics, evaluating which kids would be easily taken out by a hail of red balls (considerations included general athletic ability, low vs. high center of gravity, established cowardice in the face of hard throws), I was rocketed back to those dreaded days on the blacktop at G.W. Jr. High. I remember quaking under the gaze of a huge, blond girl who even then I knew was destined to remember eighth grade as the apogee of her life. She smiles, heaves back her strong arm, and wails the ball. Before it even begins its arc through the air I'm on the ground, quivering, arms over my head, already crying even though I haven't been hit yet.

## Taking Action

"I'm calling your gym teacher," I announced.

My children stared at me, mouths agape.

"What are you talking about?" my 10-year-old daughter said.

"You can't play dodgeball. It's cruel."

"It is not," wailed my son.

"Yes it is," I said. "It's mean! It's mean to pick on a kid because she's weak, because she can't catch a ball, or duck, or run fast enough."

The children looked at each other and then at me. Clearly, the more barbaric aspects of the game had not even penetrated their consciousness.

"Mom," my daughter said. "Please, Mom. Do not call our gym teacher. Please."

## Trying to Ban Dodgeball

But it was too late. I was already marshaling my facts. The National Association for Sport & Physical Education has issued a position paper on dodgeball, and they don't like it any more than I do. Dodgeball is not an appropriate activity for K-12 school physical education programs, says the NASPE. A game that targets and eliminates weaker kids does not help them develop confidence. While it may allow for the practice of some physical skills, there are many other activities that do this better, without using human targets. Furthermore, the only children who like dodgeball are the children who don't get hit, who don't get eliminated, who don't get wailed on. Like, for some reason, my children.

I prepared for my conversation with my children's gym teacher by learning by heart the following statement from the NASPE. "It is not appropriate to teach our children that you win by hurting others." Then I made the call. My children go to a remarkable school where community service is an actual part of the curriculum. It made no sense for dodgeball to exist there. This is a school where conflict resolution is taken so seriously that when some neighborhood toughs threw eggs at the fourth graders, the head of the lower school brought them in for a mediated encounter session. This is a school that takes very seriously the theories of Vivian Gussin Paley, author of the marvelous book on childhood social ostracism *You Can't Say You Can't Play.* I chose this school precisely because it is the polar opposite of G.W. Jr. High. The gym teacher and the head of the lower school called me back, not a little confused, especially when I explained that, while my children were enjoying themselves tremendously playing dodgeball, and that I didn't actually know of any kids who weren't, I still thought they should ban the game.

## Living Out My Fantasies

It was only while I was earnestly describing to the head of the lower school how detrimental dodgeball was to our children's developing bodies and minds, through the prism, I might add, of my experience huddling with my hands over my 11-year-old head while dozens of balls rained down on me, that I realized that what I was really trying to do was exorcise the ghosts of my own unhappy childhood. I was stirring up trouble at my children's school because 25 years ago I was miserable, and I had decided dodgeball was the very matrix of that misery, in which all the lines of force that were conspiring to crush my spirit were laid bare.

The thing is, my fantasies about being a parent always involved fighting for my unpopular child, doing for her what my own parents couldn't do for me when I was a girl. I am so ready to be that little girl's mother. I know just how to provide the proper sympathy, exactly what to say when the boys call out, "Hey, carpenter's dream!" (flat as a board, and easy to screw), or when you find a page in a slam book dedicated to you. My mother, as supportive and loving as she is, was always left somewhat befuddled and at a loss by my sufferings. "But I always had so many friends when I was a girl!" she used to say. Now that it's my turn to be the mom, maybe I overcompensate. I regale my children with tales of how I used to eat my lunch huddled over a book in a corner of the school library because no one would let me sit at their lunch table. I comfort them with stories about geeks and nerds who went on to conquer the world.

## Their Childhood, Not Mine

There's only one problem. My children are nothing like me, and they can never quite figure out why I'm laying it on so thick. They aren't living out my childhood, they're living their own. Whatever problems they might have, and they've got plenty, they're not the same ones I had. Sure, they feel sorry for me, or the me that I once was, but they don't really get it. My oldest daughter is supremely confident, secure in her position in her class and with her friends. She's *always* been popular. She was the queen bee of Gymboree. My son doesn't have her social ease, but neither does he have quite my awkwardness.

And he loves dodgeball.

Halfway through the dodgeball wars, I dropped the ball. On purpose. Whatever I think of the pedagogical value of the game, the fact is my children are happy. They like school, they like gym class. What they don't like is their mother working out her adolescent traumas by berating their gym teacher.

There are times as a parent when you realize that your job is not to be the parent you always imagined you'd be, the parent you always wished you had. Your job is to be the parent your child needs, given the particulars of his or her own life and nature. It's hard to separate your remembered childhood and its emotional legacy from the childhoods that are being lived out in your house, by your children. If you're lucky, your kids will help you make that distinction. They'll look at you, stricken, and beg you not to harangue the coach, not to harass the mother of the boy who didn't invite them to the birthday party, not to intervene to rescind the lousy trade of Yu-Gi-Oh cards they made. You want to protect them, but sometimes what you have to protect them from is the ongoing avalanche of your own childhood—crashing down on you like a hail of dodgeballs.

# Organizations to Contact

*The editors have compiled the following list of organizations concerned with the issues debated in this book. The descriptions are derived from materials provided by the organizations. All have publications or information available for interested readers. The list was compiled on the date of publication of the present volume; the information provided here may change. Be aware that many organizations take several weeks or longer to respond to inquiries, so allow as much time as possible.*

## Bully Busters

Web site: workplacebullying.org

The Bully Busters Web site offers a number of linked resources for those affected by workplace bullying and for those who want to work to eradicate it. From training courses and online surveys to advocacy efforts and sponsorship of annual "Freedom from Bullies" week, the organization addresses the many issues surrounding bullying in the workplace.

## Bully Police USA

e-mail: Brenda@jaredstory.com
Web site: www.bullypolice.org

Founded by a woman whose son committed suicide following years of bullying, Bully Police USA serves as an informational resource on antibullying legislation and activism around the country. The Web site gives grades to states based on their passage of antibullying laws and offers information on how to get such legislation introduced in other states. The organization's founders have published a book, *Bullycide in America*, and are working on a collection of antibullying essays, *Heroes in the Crowd*. Bully Police also moderates several online discussion groups devoted to bullying issues.

**Bullying Canada**
e-mail: Rfrenette@bullyingcanada.ca
Web site: bullyingcanada.ca

Bullying Canada is an online resource produced by and for Canadian youth. Bullying Canada's Web site provides stories and poems written by young people about their bullying experiences and publishes the latest news stories relating to bullying. The organization also sponsors a moderated chat room. Although the organization does not offer online counseling, it will refer site visitors to local or regional aid agencies.

**International Bullying Prevention Association (IBPA)**
P.O. Box 2288, Falmouth, MA   02536
(508) 274-8426
e-mail: info@stopbullyingworld.org
Web site: www.stopbullyingworld.org

The IBPA sponsors research into bullying prevention tactics and techniques and organizes initiatives to incorporate research-based best practices into bullying prevention programs in schools and communities. The IBPA sponsors an annual conference, posts links to the latest research, and publishes an e-newsletter. The organization's Web site also provides an extensive list of online resources, including articles, Web sites, videos, and bullying prevention materials.

**National Education Association Bullying**
**Awareness Campaign**
1201 16th Street NW, Washington, DC   20036
(202) 833-4000 • fax: (202) 822-7974
Web site: www.nea.org/schoolsafety/bullying.html

The country's largest educators' organization, the National Education Association sponsors a program called the National Bullying Awareness Campaign as part of its school safety initiative. The campaign focuses on involving all members of the educational community—administrators, teachers, school support personnel, parents, and the larger community—in the goal of eradicating bullying. The organization's Web site provides a bulleted list of specific actions groups can take to achieve this goal.

## National Organizations for Youth Safety
7371 Atlas Walk Way, #109, Gainesville, VA   20155
(703) 981-0264 • fax: (703) 754-8262
e-mail: sspavone@noys.org
Web site: www.noys.org

The mission of the National Organizations for Youth Safety is to be the premier national youth health and safety coalition. To that end, the member groups sponsor programs related to traffic safety, substance abuse, safe parties, and sexual health. The coalition considers bullying to be an important youth safety issue and helps sponsor activities related to the federal government's Stop Bullying Now initiative.

## National Youth Violence Prevention Resource Center
Web site: www.safeyouth.org/scripts/topics/bullying.asp

Sponsored by the U.S. Centers for Disease Control and Prevention, the National Youth Violence Prevention Resource Center was established in the aftermath of the 1999 Columbine school shootings and is intended "to serve as a user-friendly, single point of access to potentially life-saving information about youth violence and prevention and intervention strategies for the general public." In addition to information on bullying, the center also provides information on alcohol abuse, dating violence, depression, and school violence. Publications include fact sheets, PowerPoint presentations, federal reports, and even comic strips.

## Operation Respect
2 Penn Plaza, 6th Floor, New York, NY   10121
(212) 904-5243
e-mail: info@operationrespect.org
Web site: www.dontlaugh.org

Founded by Peter Yarrow of the folk singing group Peter, Paul, and Mary, Operation Respect is devoted to assuring that children have a safe and bully-free environment for learning. Primarily focused on curriculum development, Operation Respect has developed Don't Laugh at Me (DLAM) programs—one for early elementary years, one for middle school—to be used in educational settings. Copies of the DLAM programs may be requested free of charge via an online form.

## PACER Kids Against Bullying
8161 Normandale Blvd., Bloomington, MN   55437
(952) 838-9000
e-mail: bullying411@pacer.org
Web site: www.pacerkidsagainstbullying.org

The PACER Center is a parent resource center that primarily serves children with disabilities but also develops antibullying programs for all children. PACER sponsors National Bullying Prevention Awareness Week each October, offering schools, parents, and students a number of materials and activities—including a coloring book, poster contest, puppet role plays, and lesson plans. The Web site includes a number of bullying prevention videos aimed at young people, as well as coloring pages and word games. Many of the publications deal specifically with bullying issues particular to children with disabilities.

## Peaceful Schools International
P.O. Box 660, Annapolis Royal, Nova Scotia
Canada   B0S 1A0
(902) 532-1111 • fax: (902) 532-1283
e-mail: info@peacefulschoolsinternational.org
Web site: peacefulschoolsinternational.org

Peaceful Schools International is a worldwide nonprofit membership organization that serves as a clearinghouse for ideas related to creating nonviolent schools. More than 250 member schools agree to abide by the organization's founding principles, which include sponsoring peace education initiatives, developing schoolwide conflict resolution programs, and providing continuing education in nonviolence issues for school staff. Peaceful Schools International publishes a monthly e-newsletter and offers a number of print publications, including the comprehensive Peace in Action Toolkit for schools interested in incorporating the organization's principles into daily life.

## Stop Bullying Now

e-mail: comments@hrsa.gov
Web site: www.stopbullyingnow.hrsa.gov

Sponsored by the federal Health Resources and Services Administration, this Web site is aimed at students ages nine to thirteen and is part of the federal government's national Take a Stand, Lend a Hand, Stop Bullying Now! campaign. The Web site offers downloadable ringtones, webisodes, online games, answers to questions about bullying, and bullying prevention resources for youth leaders. For parents and professionals, the Web site also offers links to curriculum materials, public service announcements, and other online resources. The entire site—for both adults and children—is available in both English and Spanish.

## Stop Violence

(816) 753-8002
e-mail: svcinfo@stop-violence.org
Web site: www.stop-violence.org

Stop Violence is part of Synergy Services, a Kansas City–based nonprofit organization. The program has been involved in bullying prevention since 1990 and has developed a number of antibullying programs, including the comprehensive Get Connected program and the Step Up program specifically aimed at preventing female bullying. This eight-part program offers facilitators resources on cliques, body image, conflict resolution, and other issues. Program participants are encouraged to keep journals and participate in discussions. Stop

Violence's online store offers these curriculum materials for sale, as well as magnets, buttons, stickers, and t-shirts that promote kindness and discourage bullying.

**Words Can Heal**
P.O. Box 5336, New York, NY   10185
(212) 245-5345
e-mail: wordscanheal@wordscanheal.org
Web site: www.wordscanheal.org

Words Can Heal is a national media and education initiative promoting the value of positive speech. Aimed at both adults and youth, Words Can Heal has found support among a number of politicians and celebrities, including Tom Cruise, Bob Dole, Goldie Hawn, and Joss Stone. The campaign uses posters, television ads, newsletters, and other media to discourage gossip and verbal put-downs and enhance interpersonal communication. Educational curriculum materials as well as a handbook and kit are available for purchase on the organization's Web site.

# For Further Research

## Books

Bonnie Burton, *Girls Against Girls: Why We Are Mean to Each Other and How We Can Change*. San Francisco: Orange Avenue, 2009.

Barbara Coloroso, *The Bully, the Bullied, and the Bystander: From Preschool to High School—How Parents and Teachers Can Help Break the Cycle of Violence*. New York: HarperResource, 2004.

Evelyn M. Field, *Bully Blocking: Six Secrets to Help Children Deal with Teasing and Bullying*. London: Kingsley, 2007.

Olivia Gardner, *Letters to a Bullied Girl: Messages of Healing and Hope*. New York: Harper, 2008.

Joel David Haber, *Bullyproof Your Child for Life: Protect Your Child from Teasing, Taunting, and Bullying for Good*. New York: Perigee, 2007.

Robin M. Kowalski, *Cyber Bullying: Bullying in the Digital Age*. Malden, MA: Blackwell, 2008.

Susan Lipkins, *Preventing Hazing: How Parents, Teachers, and Coaches Can Stop the Violence, Harassment, and Humiliation*. San Francisco: Jossey-Bass, 2006.

Robyn MacEachern, *Cyberbullying: Deal with It and Ctrl Alt Delete It*. Toronto: Lorimer, 2008.

Ken Rigby, *Children and Bullying: How Parents and Educators Can Reduce Bullying at School*. Malden, MA: Blackwell, 2008.

Ian Rivers, *Bullying: A Handbook for Educators and Parents*. Westport, CT: Praeger, 2007.

Joanne Scaglione, *Bully-Proofing Children: A Practical, Hands-On Guide to Stop Bullying*. Lanham, MD: Rowman & Littlefield, 2006.

Susan Sprague, *Coping with Cliques*. Oakland, CA: New Harbinger, 2008.

Barbara Sprung, *The Anti-Bullying and Teasing Book for Preschool Classrooms*. Beltsville, MD: Gryphon House, 2005.

Julie Ann Wambach, *Battles Between Somebodies and Nobodies: Stop Abuse of Rank at Work and at Home*. Scottsdale, AZ: Brookside, 2008.

Rosalind Wiseman, *Queen Bee Moms and Kingpin Dads: Dealing with the Difficult Parents in Your Child's Life*. New York: Three Rivers Press, 2006.

## Periodicals

Madonna Behen, "Stamp Out Bullying," *Woman's Day*, October 2, 2007.

Bruce Bower, "No-Fight Zones," *Science News*, September 1, 2007.

Leigh Buchanan, "The Bully Rulebook: How to Deal with Jerks," *Inc.*, February 2007.

Kira Cochrane, "Who Would Be a Teenager Now?" *New Statesman*, March 3, 2008.

Margaret Fuhrer, "Don't Bully, Dance," *Dance Magazine*, May 2008.

William L. Hawkins, "Bullies Among Us," *Christian Century*, May 29, 2007.

Jane N. Kim, "The Cubicle Bully," *Scientific American Mind*, June 2008.

Katherine Lee, "The Big Bully Problem," *Working Mother*, October 2007.

Cindy Long, "Silencing Cyberbullies," *NEA Today*, May 2008.

Kristen Mascia, "She Battles Bullies in Her Son's Memory," *People*, September 15, 2008.

Leslie Harris O'Hanlon, "Hostile Halls," *Current Health 2*, October 2006.

Selena Roberts, "Jocks Against Bullies," *Sports Illustrated*, July 7, 2008.

Fran Smith, "Going After Cyberbullies," *Prevention*, September 2006.

*USA Today* Magazine, "Gifted Teens Vulnerable to Effects of Bullying," September 2007.

# Index

Coloroso, Barbara (parenting expert), 71
Columbine High School shootings, 12
Confidence
    loss of, 24, 49, 59, 61
    refinding, 83–84
Confronting a bully, 52–53
Counseling for depression, 61
Critical behavior, 49–50
Cruel behavior of bullies, 44, 75
Crying (from being bullied), 24, 29, 35, 36, 40, 44, 48
Cyberbullying, 64–67

**D**

Dance students
    bullying/harassment of, 23–25
    stereotyping of, 25–26
Death from bullying, 34–37, 64–65, 69, 70
    *See also* Suicide
Depression
    battling with/overcoming, 78
    of teachers, 60–62
    of teenagers, 30–31
    treatment options, 81
Despair, of students, 29
Disabled people, bullying of, 12, 13, 15
Discouraging behavior, 49–50
Dodgeball, 86–91
Don't suffer in silence (Web site), 45–46
Dowd, Maureen, 67
Drugs (pharmaceutical) for depression, 61–62
Dysfunctional families, 64

**E**

Eating disorders, 41
Elementary school students, 12, 17–22
E-mail messages/rejections, 28, 29, 66
Embarrassment of students, 23, 25, 26
Exposing bullies, by victims, 45–46

**F**

Family background, of bullies/victims, 35, 39, 60, 64, 75
Father, concern for bullied child, 30
Fear
    adults, of bully, 52
    children/students, 28–29
    cyberbullying, 65
    students, 25
Ford, Gabrielle (bullying victim), 12, 15
Forgiveness, by bullied student, 33
Friedreich'ts ataxia, 12

**G**

Getting over being bullied, 38
Gold, Rhee, 23–26
*Good Morning America* (TV show), 68–69
Goulston, Mark, 51–57
Group behavior, of students, 39
Guidance counselor, encouragement from, 77–78
Guilty feelings, 46, 62